EMOTIONAL AND BEHAVIOURAL DIFFICULTIES

Theory to practice

*Paul Cooper, Colin J. Smith
and Graham Upton*

D0538524

ROUTLEDGE

London and New York

First published 1994
by Routledge
11 New Fetter Lane, London EC4P 4EE

Simultaneously published in the USA and Canada
by Routledge
29 West 35th Street, New York, NY 10001

Typeset in Palatino by LaserScript, Mitcham, Surrey
Printed and bound in Great Britain by
Biddles Ltd, Guildford and King's Lynn

British Library Cataloguing in Publication Data
A catalogue record for this book is available from the British Library.

Library of Congress Cataloging in Publication Data
Cooper, Paul, 1955–
Emotional and behavioural difficulties: theory to practice/
Paul Cooper, Colin J. Smith, and Graham Upton.
p. cm.
Includes bibliographical references and index.
1. Problem children – Education – Great Britain.
2. Behavior modification – Great Britain.
3. Classroom management – Great Britain.
I. Smith, Colin, 1938–   . II. Upton, Graham, 1944–
III. Title.
LC4803.G7C66   1994
371.93'0941 – dc20   93-25943
                                                        CIP

ISBN 0–415–07198–4 (hbk)
ISBN 0–415–07199–2 (pbk)

CONTENTS

CONTENTS

INTRODUCTION

Why this book is necessary

Behavioural problems in schools are a perennial area of concern for teachers, local authorities, policy makers and the public at large. This is demonstrated in the media interest which has been devoted to the subject, the publication of the Elton Report (DES, 1989a), as well as in reports from teacher unions and professional associations (e.g. AMMA, 1986). In spite of the emphasis placed by the Education Reform Act (1988) on the entitlement of all pupils to a 'broad and balanced' school curriculum, evidence suggests sharp increases in the numbers of pupils who are excluded from schools (and therefore, their entitlement to the National Curriculum) as a result of behavioural problems (ILEA, 1990; Merrick and Manuel, 1991; Pyke, 1991). Research also suggests that pupils become increasingly disaffected from school and critical of their teachers as they advance through formal schooling (Keys and Fernandes, 1993). Furthermore, there is some suggestion that the already considerable difficulties which many schools face in preventing and alleviating disaffection and problem behaviour are being exacerbated as a result of measures introduced in the Education Reform Act, 1988 (Woods, 1990b; Pyke, 1991). The imposition by government of crude performance indicators, such as rates of public examination success and truancy, may well lead some schools to abandon pupils who are likely to bring performance scores down. Individual teachers, too, might be increasingly inclined to seek the removal of disruptive pupils from their classes, rather than attempting to deal with problem behaviour in the classroom. This would be an understandable response if teachers were to

1

feel that their own performance, and possibly their job security, were to depend, in part at least, on the quality of pupil behaviour observed in their classrooms by appraisers. On the other hand, the provisions of the Children Act (1989) make it a duty of schools and teachers to take careful account of pupils' welfare needs and, where necessary, pass information to Social Service Departments. This places teachers in a key position, with regard to pupils' welfare needs. In the light of these circumstances, there has perhaps never been a worse time than the present to be a pupil experiencing emotional and behavioural difficulties in school, or a more challenging time to be a teacher faced with 'difficult' pupils. This makes the need for a book such as this all the more urgent.

A brief consideration of the history of educational responses to emotional and behavioural difficulties shows a growing realisation of the importance of the context in which they occur, and the way in which the role of the mainstream teacher has come to demand expertise in dealing with emotional and behavioural difficulties.

The origins of modern approaches to dealing with school pupils with emotional and behavioural difficulties lie in the early part of the twentieth century. The earliest approaches were based on medical, psychological and psychiatric models. These approaches gave rise to the non-punitive, 'therapeutic' methods, which flourished in an initially small number of residential establishments (Bridgeland, 1971). Until educational psychology became a powerful force in education in the 1960s and 1970s, expertise in dealing with pupils with emotional and behavioural difficulties was located in the province of the medical fraternity, who determined their 'treatment' and placement (Laslett, 1983). This transfer of behavioural problems from the educational to the medical arena led to the establishment of segregated, often residential, provision for pupils with emotional and behavioural difficulties. The growth of educational psychology, however, brought with it a challenge to medical dominance and the assertion of the view that the placement and treatment of school pupils should be made on educational grounds by educationists.

The advent of educational psychology coincided with the beginning of the move towards policies advocating the integration of pupils with special educational needs into mainstream settings (DES, 1978; Education Acts, 1980, 1981), which demand the provision of staff with specialist skills in mainstream schools, and the widening of subject teachers' skill base to include the ability to cope effectively with pupils with emotional and behavioural difficulties. At the same time, these changes have been accompanied by a move towards a 'service' view of education, whereby pupils and their parents are seen as 'clients', and teachers and schools are seen as service providers. Along with this view, clearly endorsed in the Education Reform Act (1988), has come an increasing emphasis on pupils and parents as consumers, with rights to minimum expectations. It is suggested that these changes reflect the growing emphasis in theoretical approaches to emotional and behavioural difficulties, on the need to consult pupils and their families, rather than seeing them as objects to be manipulated by distant experts. This development is demonstrated in the move by educational psychologists away from highly mechanistic behavioural approaches, towards more interactive modes of treatment (see Varma, 1990).

This brief history (expanded more fully in Chapter 2) shows how changes in the philosophy and organisational arrangements concerning emotional and behavioural difficulties in schools have led to dramatic changes, with responsibility for responding to emotional and behavioural difficulties moving from the position of being completely outside the educational realm to being firmly within it. However, whilst the job of teaching has come to place increasing demands on teachers' skills in dealing with pupils with emotional and behavioural difficulties, there is evidence to suggest that teachers feel ill-equipped to meet this challenge. Teachers in general are unprepared by their initial training, and by in-service training arrangements for dealing with emotional and behavioural difficulties (DES, 1989a, 1985), and specialist teachers in the field have been shown to place their requirement for further training in the area high on their list of priorities (Cooper, Smith and Upton, 1990, 1991).

This book is intended to provide teachers and teacher trainers with a concise and practical guide to some of the major approaches which can be used to understand and deal with emotional and behavioural difficulties in schools. This is a guide which offers readers an accessible account of practical approaches to problem behaviour and their theoretical underpinnings. It is aimed at readers with professional training in education and practical experience of teaching. The book is intended to serve three related purposes:

1 as a resource for in-service training and professional development;
2 as a tool for schools to use in establishing whole school approaches to dealing with emotional and behavioural difficulties;
3 as a guide to individual teachers, and related professionals, engaging in personal study and reflection on emotional and behavioural difficulties.

It is argued that teachers need to know about the range of possible intervention strategies as well as understand the theoretical underpinnings of these strategies. Such theoretical knowledge is essential in the development of consistent and coherent whole school approaches to emotional and behavioural difficulties.

TEACHERS' CRAFT KNOWLEDGE AND EDUCATIONAL THEORY

Underlying this book is the view that teaching is an enormously complex process. Effective teaching depends on highly complex skills that are developed through experience and reflection on practice (Clark and Peterson, 1986; Calderhead, 1987; Brown and McIntyre, 1993). A highly pervasive influence on the development of teachers' teaching skills is the practical experience they gain of what works in the classroom. This is not to say that there is no room for theory in teaching. On the contrary, educational theory has a great deal to offer teachers, since it contributes to the second important influence on teachers' skill development: the ways in which they think about their classroom practice.

A useful way of thinking about skill development in teaching is to see it as a hypothesis testing process (McIntyre, 1991), whereby teachers try out practical techniques which they have learned about from a variety of sources, such as from colleagues, from their own experience as pupils, from college lectures and from their reading. The key process here is one of reflection, whereby teachers continually scrutinise and evaluate their own practice, and seek ways of improving their mastery of their craft. Knowledge of the theory underlying practical teaching can be of use to the reflection process in a number of ways. First, knowledge of explanatory theory helps us to understand how and why a particular teaching technique works, and in so doing provides a language with which teaching can be explored. The language can also be used by teachers to articulate their own implicit thinking which underlies their successful practice. The articulation of such 'craft knowledge' (Desforges and McNamara, 1979) puts it into a form that enables it to be shared with co-professionals (Brown and McIntyre, 1993). Benefits from this sharing process include the refinement and development of ideas and practices, and with this, improvements in teachers' confidence in their abilities and skills. Second, theoretical explanations, through the abstraction of basic principles, help us to understand how a particular technique might be transferred to and from other situations (teaching and non-teaching). For example, in the present book, we see how theoretical insights from family therapy can be employed in the school context (see Chapter 6). Third, theory can be used by the practising teacher as a means of formulating new hypotheses to be employed in their own working context. This book, then, should be seen as a source book, which offers a wide range of hypotheses for teachers to consider when dealing with issues relating to emotional and behavioural difficulties, as well as providing a stimulus for hypothesis generation. We hope that, out of the meeting that takes place between the ideas contained here and the practical knowledge that teachers bring with them to the book, will come fruitful and open discussion about practical issues.

DEALING WITH EMOTIONAL AND BEHAVIOURAL DIFFICULTIES: SOME COMMON THEMES

As far as possible, the contents of this book have been presented in as dispassionate a way as possible. We do not intend to show favour to any of the techniques presented above the others. What is clear, however, is that different techniques are appropriate to different situations, and it is the wide diversity of situations that give rise to emotional and behavioural difficulties which explains the concomitant diversity of approaches. Having said this, there are certain important commonalities that can be traced throughout the book, and can be seen to unite modern approaches to emotional and behavioural difficulties in schools. These commonalities can be summarised as follows:

1 *Whether they like it or not, teachers do have an effect on emotional and behavioural difficulties.* Teachers are not simply victims of the social and psychological forces that produce emotional and behavioural difficulties. Whilst they are influenced by the context in which they operate, they are also an influence upon it, and thus upon others within it. They can either make their influence contribute to the development of emotional and behavioural difficulties or they can try to bring their influence to bear on their prevention or remediation. There is no neutral ground here. Each theoretical explanation for the origins of emotional and behavioural difficulties produces its own set of solutions, some of which the teacher can implement in the classroom (e.g. behavioural approaches and classroom management strategies), others which may require the calling in of outside agencies (e.g. situations requiring intervention in the family situation and circumstances requiring the intervention of a clinical psychologist or psychiatrist).

2 *All* pupils benefit from circumstances that are conducive to the prevention of emotional and behavioural difficulties in schools. Circumstances that are conducive to the prevention of emotional and behavioural difficulties are also conducive to effective teaching and learning. It is important to realise that the nature of curriculum content and the method of its delivery influence pupil behaviour.

3 *All* effective approaches to emotional and behavioural difficulties require teachers to value pupils and to respect the pupil perspective. In different ways, each approach can be seen to pay close attention to pupils' perceptions of their own situations, and to create environments which are in harmony with pupils' requirements for positive social experiences. This is true of the more directive approaches, such as the

behavioural and classroom management strategies, which respond to pupils' often stated preference for well-ordered classroom environments; it is also true of the less directive and more humanistic approaches, such as psychodynamic and ecosystemic approaches, which involve gaining access to pupils' particular and individual perceptions. All approaches involve a commitment to providing pupils with positive, rewarding experiences of schooling rather than negative and punitive experiences.

4 The potential for the success of *all* approaches is optimised when they are carried out within the context of a whole school policy. Staff and pupils benefit from the security and direction provided by a consistent and coherent school-wide approach to dealing with behavioural problems. Staff derive support from clarity of purpose and common direction, whilst pupils derive security from consistency of staff expectations.

OVERVIEW OF CHAPTERS

Chapters 1 and 2 expand the theme of the present chapter, by describing the context in which emotional and behavioural difficulties are to be considered throughout the book. Chapter 1 deals with the nature and development of emotional and behavioural difficulties. Different ways of conceptualising emotional and behavioural problems are considered and issues of causation are dealt with; the evolution of terminology is discussed and contrasting approaches are illustrated. Chapter 2 focuses on educational responses to behavioural problems and illustrates the way in which changing views on the nature and development of emotional and behavioural difficulties are reflected in changes in the nature and patterns of educational provision for pupils with such difficulties.

Chapters 3 to 6 are devoted to the description and discussion of different approaches to emotional and behavioural problems in schools, their theoretical bases and practical applications. Chapter 3 considers the importance of interpersonal relationships in the development and treatment of behavioural problems. This chapter focuses on ways in which counselling and therapy techniques, based on psychoanalytic theory, can help us to understand some of the ways in which emotional and behavioural difficulties can arise and be treated. Chapter 4 deals with approaches to behaviour problems that are based on applications of learning theory from the perspective of behavioural psychology. Whilst Chapter 3 sounds a cautious note, drawing a clear distinction between insights that teachers can employ in their daily work with pupils and those levels of psychotherapy that are the proper concern of professional psychotherapists alone, Chapter 4 provides practical information about the procedures which classroom teachers can employ in their own classrooms, in order to shape the behaviour of their pupils. It should be clear from these chapters that whilst behavioural and therapeutic approaches appear to be based on entirely different theoretical principles, which produce contrasting practices, they are not to be seen as necessarily contradictory. Rather, these two approaches can be seen as complementary, each being appropriate to particular kinds of problems. Chapter 5 explores the importance of the broader social context surrounding the emergence of emotional and behavioural difficulties, such as the family. Drawing on insights from family therapy and systemic theory, this chapter shows how solutions to apparently intractable emotional and behavioural difficulties can be found in unexpected places (both inside and outside schools) when an 'ecosystemic' approach is adopted. Chapter 6 is concerned with classroom management. After dealing with the conceptual underpinnings of classroom management, practical management strategies are discussed. Central to this chapter is the view that an understanding of the dynamics of social interaction can be harnessed in the development of effective classroom management strategies.

The next two chapters draw on research evidence which indicates the types of policy measures which schools might adopt in the response to the problems presented by pupils with emotional and behavioural difficulties. These chapters show that behavioural methods and measures concerned with the quality of interpersonal and social relationships can influence the quality of pupils' behaviour and affective states in schools. A particular focus of Chapter 7 is the way in which pupils' perceptions of their circumstances can be employed in the development of an appropriate policy. Chapter 8 shows how whole school policies can be developed, with practical exemplification. Emphasis is placed on the importance of consultation and evaluation procedures in the production of development plans.

Chapter 9, the final chapter, focuses on school effectiveness and the ways in which teachers and staff groups can systematically make use of the wide range of possible solutions to emotional and behavioural difficulties presented in this book, through close reference to the particularities of their working situation.

Part I

CONSIDERING PROBLEMS

OVERVIEW

In this part of the book, we examine the different theories which have sought to explain the nature of emotional and behavioural difficulties, and which have provided the rationale for educational practice in responding to them. In considering the problems presented by pupils with emotional and behavioural difficulties, there has been a distinct move away from the simple ascription of problems to individual psychopathology, towards an acceptance that the definition of emotional and behavioural difficulties, like other special educational needs, is a complex, interactive process. In delineating this process we look first at the nature and development of behaviour problems.

We begin by establishing the inevitably subjective character of attempts to define behaviour problems and reflecting upon sociological perspectives on deviance and labelling. This leads to consideration of implications for schools as organisations, particularly with regard to the ways in which they think about rules and the ways in which they deal with those who do not conform to them. Medical, behavioural and ecosystemic models of behaviour and misbehaviour are explained, and arguments are advanced for a broader conceptualisation of behaviour problems in schools, which takes greater account of the human being's capacity to change and develop and assume more institutional responsibility for interventions which foster such changes.

Theoretical approaches to such intervention are further explored through tracing the history and development of educational provision for pupils whose behaviour has presented problems for themselves and their teachers. Early perceptions of

13

'maladjustment' defined problem and treatment in medical terms, drawing especially on the perspectives of psychoanalysis and psychotherapy. Examples of early pioneering work in residential schools, based on these disciplines, are discussed before considering the changes in thinking which have encouraged a more psycho-educational approach in special schools and units, and which has focused attention on school organisation and management of the curriculum and emphasised the responsibilities of mainstream schools in adapting policies to meet the needs of pupils with emotional and behavioural difficulties.

This part of the book sets the context and provides the background for the more detailed discussion of the theories which underpin particular intervention strategies, which are examined in Part II.

1

THE NATURE AND
DEVELOPMENT OF
BEHAVIOUR
PROBLEMS

Historically, attempts to understand and deal with behavioural difficulties in schools have tended to focus on the pupil as being, and having, the problem. This is not surprising given the responsibility of teachers to create effective learning environments for whole classes of pupils and for which there is a need to maintain a certain degree of order and discipline in the classroom. Behaviour problems constitute a direct threat to that responsibility and, at the same time, may be seen as reflecting poorly on the teacher's professional skills and status in the eyes of colleagues, parents and pupils. From this perspective, it is understandable that teachers react negatively to the occurrence of behaviour problems, and that such problems have been conceptualised in ways which ascribe primary responsibility for the problems to the pupils.

This tendency towards pupil blame is reinforced by the fact that some instances of behavioural difficulty are initiated by pupils and have their origin in the disturbed, disturbing or aggressive behaviour of these pupils. Behaviour problems in schools sometimes reflect underlying emotional difficulties arising out of factors such as a difficult family background or physical or sexual abuse; some pupils behave in disruptive ways in school because they are the norm in a pupil's family or social sub-group and their life, both in and out of school, is characterised by acts of anti-social behaviour, violence and aggression. Hard data are not available which allow this group to be distinguished from the larger group of pupils whose behaviour at some time or other in their school career may result in them being identified as having behaviour problems, but it probably represents a small proportion of that group.

The difficulties which teachers face in creating effective learning environments and at the same time recognising and meeting individual emotional needs and dealing with discipline problems are considerable. Recognition of these difficulties led, in Britain, to the creation of the official Committee of Enquiry chaired by Lord Elton 'to recommend action to the Government, local authorities, voluntary bodies, governors, headteachers, teachers and parents aimed at securing the orderly atmosphere necessary in school for effective teaching and learning to take place' (DES, 1989a, p. 11). At the same time it is important to recognise the complex nature of behaviour problems which renders simple ascriptions of blame for their occurrence to pupils inadequate.

PERCEPTIONS OF REALITY

Fundamental to the understanding of behaviour problems is recognition that their identification, any description of them and any attempt to identify reasons for their occurrence involves a high degree of subjectivity. Speed (1991) notes that 'realism has been the epistemological stance traditionally, though often implicitly, taken by the helping professions' and from which position 'for psychiatrist and psychoanalysts for example, a discoverable reality, be it the inner world of the patient or psychiatric illness, is assumed to exist and be discernible' (p. 396). But, for some time convincing arguments (see, for example, Berger and Luckman, 1966; Watzlawick, 1984) have been advanced which suggest that we can never know objective reality. Rather, different people place different interpretations on what happens around them, according to their view of the world, and thus *construct* their own views of reality. Extreme positions have been taken on this issue but, as time has passed, more balanced views have begun to emerge and Speed (1991) advocates the value of what she describes as a 'co-constructivist' position which accepts that 'a structured reality exists but recognises that the reality is constructed or mediated in the sense that different aspects are highlighted according to ideas that individuals or groups have about it' (p. 401).

16

This position has particular pertinence to behaviour problems in schools, where pupils and teachers, for example, may have greatly divergent views on what has happened and why. While teachers often complain of the irrational nature of problem behaviour and decry the extent to which it prevents them from teaching effectively, researchers such as Reid (1985) and Cronk (1987), who have explored the perceptions held by disruptive pupils, have commonly found that they often view their acts of disruption as rational and justifiable responses to poor teaching. Similarly, different teachers frequently hold very different views about whether or not a pupil is a behaviour problem. This does not mean that one is right and the other is wrong; rather it reflects the interactional nature of behaviour problems and the different values and attitudes which individuals hold. Different teachers (and schools) have different standards for, and expectations of, the behaviour of their pupils whereby differences in reported behaviour may reflect differences in the degree to which difficult behaviour is tolerated.

Further insight into the subjective nature of behaviour problems has been provided by social theorists who, since the 1960s, have focused on the concept of deviance and proposed a new orientation which has been commonly referred to as the 'labelling theory' or the 'interactionist' approach. Instead of focusing on individual pathology (as is traditional with the medical model) the interactionist perspective has focused on social processes and the way in which individuals come to be labelled as deviant (or mentally ill, or delinquent, or maladjusted). An early advocate of this approach, Kitsuse (1962), argued that 'deviance may be conceived of as a process by which the members of a group, community, or society (1) interpret behaviour as deviant, (2) define persons who so behave as a certain kind of deviant, and (3) accord them the treatment considered appropriate' (p. 248). Hargreaves *et al.* (1975) echoed these comments in their description of the approach as being characterised by two features:

a First deviance is seen as a question of social definition. Deviance does not arise when a person commits certain kinds of act. Rather, deviance arises when some other person(s) defines that act as deviant.

b Second, deviance is seen as a relative phenomenon. If a deviant act is an act that breaks some rules, then since rules vary between different cultures, subcultures and groups, acts which are deviant (i.e. which break rules) in one culture, subculture or group may not be deviant in another culture, subculture or group.

In relation to behaviour problems in schools such views are helpful in understanding issues such as the disproportionate number of boys and pupils of ethnic minority origins who are identified as being behaviour problems and referred for special educational placement (see Cooper, Smith and Upton, 1990). Davies (1984), for example, has looked from this perspective at gender differences which exist in the identification, incidence and nature of behaviour problems in schools, and raised important questions about the definition of good and bad behaviour and its treatment. In their response to a questionnaire which asked them to indicate what traits they thought were exhibited by well-adjusted, reasonably successful pupils, teachers displayed what Davies (1979) labels as a unisex view of the good pupil, describing their ideal pupil in terms which were very similar for boys and girls (helpful, responsible, independent, hardworking, etc.). However, once the teachers began to talk about the behaviour of deviant pupils, clear differences emerged based on sex-role stereotypes. Thus 'teachers will apparently expect and condone a certain amount of aggressive behaviour from boys, and even sexual harassment towards the girls' but 'they castigate overt expressions of femininity or sexual allure, and are quick to label girls "sluts" and "bitches"' (J. Davies, 1987, p. 145).

From this perspective, it is interesting also to consider the relationship between problem behaviour and the structures which schools create to control that behaviour. School rules, for example, are ostensibly framed to control pupil behaviour, but it can be argued that the rules actually create the problems. Thus, a policy on school uniform creates problems in terms of the children who do not abide by that rule, while the absence of such a policy would mean that no problems would arise in this area.

Taken to its logical extreme, this would imply that a school with no rules would have no problem behaviour. While this may be true, social organisations like schools clearly need rules. The number of rules required in any organisation and the nature of those rules is, however, in the hands of the people who control that organisation – in schools, the headmaster and the teaching staff. Rules in schools are usually justified in terms of them being necessary responses to pupil behaviour; labelling theory inverts this argument and suggests the need for a careful consideration in any school of the number of rules that are necessary and desirable. In particular, it raises the question of whether schools frequently generate too many rules and thus create problems about issues which may not be vital to the educative process.

QUESTIONS OF CAUSATION

Over time, the occurrence of behaviour problems has been associated with a wide range of factors (see Charlton and David, 1989, for a succinct review of relevant research). Foremost have been family influences, ranging from poor housing conditions and low social class background through to more sophisticated elements of disrupted parent–child relationships and parental discord and disturbance. Equally strongly, a variety of personal factors have been associated with behaviour problems ranging from poor physical development through low intellectual and academic ability to such syndromes as minimal brain dysfunction and hyperactivity. There is little doubt that factors of this nature can, and do, exert a strong influence over the behaviour of pupils in school, and that some children bring with them to school individual life histories and family pathologies which render positive classroom behaviour highly unlikely.

However, until very recently, the emphasis in attempts to understand the incidence of behaviour problems has been almost too heavily focused on matters of individual and family pathology with little attention being given to the extent to which schools may exacerbate, and sometimes actually cause, behaviour problems. The influence of schools in general, and teachers in particular, on the behaviour of their pupils has recently been highlighted by a number of studies (see, for example, Reynolds and Murgatroyd, 1974; Rutter *et al.*, 1979;

Mortimore *et al.*, 1983). This issue is discussed fully in Chapter 9 and it is not appropriate to repeat that discussion here. It is important, however, to note that it is now widely accepted that schools do make marked differences in the behaviour patterns of their pupils and to consider the significance of this for the understanding of behaviour problems. The clear implication of this is that the tendency which has been referred to above, to focus attention solely on individual pupils, cannot be justified. Behaviour can be highly situation specific and it is not uncommon for pupils, and teachers, to behave very differently from one lesson to the next; nor is it uncommon for pupils' behaviour at home to be very different from that which they display at school. It is necessary to recognise that classroom behaviour must represent an *interaction* between pupils and teachers and that this, in turn, is influenced by the general ethos of the school. The role which teachers play in the generation of behaviour problems cannot be denied and, in fairness to pupils, intervention may sometimes need to be focused on the teacher rather than the pupil.

TERMINOLOGY

The tendency to ascribe blame to pupils is clearly reflected in the ways in which we refer to such problems. Almost all of the terms which we use now, and have used in the past, to describe problems related to social and emotional behaviour, imply that the child is at fault. The formal definition of emotional and behavioural difficulties in Britain (see Circular 23/89, DES, 1989b) refers to 'children who set up barriers between themselves and their learning environment through inappropriate, aggressive, bizarre or withdrawn behaviour' and who 'have developed a range of strategies for dealing with day-to-day experiences that are inappropriate and impede normal personal and social development, and make it difficult for them to learn'. Similarly, from 1944 to 1981 the official term which was used in Britain to refer to these children was 'maladjusted' which, together with other terms such as 'disturbed', 'disruptive' and 'psychiatrically ill', all assume that it is the child who is maladjusted, disturbed or disruptive or who is psychiatrically ill. They suggest that the problem resides within the child and that it is the child who must be treated and cured.

As noted above, while such a description may be appropriately applied to some pupils who are identified as being behaviour problems, it is not appropriate to all such cases. A number of writers have criticised the use of such narrow terms because of the extent to which they ignore the social context in which human behaviour occurs, and the possibility of the locus of responsibility for the problem residing within the social systems of the family and the school rather than within the child. In 1972 Ravenette criticised the use of the term 'maladjustment' on the grounds that a child may be labelled as maladjusted not because of his or her own needs but because of the needs of the school, and argued that a distinction should be made between the disturbed and the disturbing child, on the basis that many children attract attention in the first instance because they are disturbing to teachers; whether they are disturbed in themselves is another matter. Fifteen years later Galloway and Goodwin (1987, p. 15) argued similarly in favour of the term 'disturbing':

> By definition, children who are called maladjusted or disturbed attract these labels because they have disturbed adults. The adult's disturbance may be at the level of frustration or anxiety at not 'getting through to' the child, or it may be sheer physical fear of violence. The term 'disturbing' implies a recognition of the children's effects on adults while the terms maladjusted and disturbed are too often taken to imply psychological or social characteristics in the child.

However, such pleas have had little impact on official thinking and even less on the language of the school staffroom where less formal terms, such as 'nutter' and 'heller', are perhaps even more direct in their attribution of responsibility. It is not clear why such terms have been so resistant to change, although terms such as those referred to above have a powerful appeal in that they can be seen to function as what Szasz (1972) in his classic study of mental illness referred to as 'social tranquillisers'. By focusing the blame for the behaviour problem on the pupil they remove the need to question the value of school structures and regimes. Any child who refuses to accept or conform to the values that have been built into the school can be readily explained away as being maladjusted or disturbed.

THEORETICAL APPROACHES

Theoretical approaches to understanding behaviour problems have also similarly tended to have an individual focus. To some extent the reason for this is that the earliest attempts to intervene and provide specialist help for children and adults with emotional problems were almost all of medical origin (Kanner, 1962). Subsequently, much of the early theorising was medically oriented as is reflected in the use of concepts such as causes, symptoms, diagnosis and treatment (all medical terms). In assessing the importance of the medical influence due credit must be given for the extent to which this produced a more caring, humane approach to the treatment and understanding of people experiencing emotional difficulties. For, instead of describing such a person as 'possessed' or 'mad' he (or she) was seen instead as a

> human being who at the present time is behaving in a self-defeating and/or needlessly anti-social manner and who will most probably continue to do so in the future, and, although he is partially creating or causing (and in this sense is responsible for) his aberrant behaviour, he is still not to be condemned for creating it but is to be helped to overcome it.
>
> (Ellis, 1967, p. 445)

Over time, many authors have questioned the value of an illness model to refer to what they argue cannot be readily conceived of as illness, but the arch-protagonist in the generation of this debate was an American psychiatrist, Thomas Szasz. In a paper titled 'The myth of mental illness' (1960), Szasz launched a controversy which has gathered momentum throughout the 1960s and 1970s. In this article, and in a subsequent book with the same title (Szasz, 1972), Szasz challenged medical domination of the field and questioned the very basis of their understanding – the medical model. The essence of Szasz's argument is caught in the following quotation:

I have tried to show that the notion of mental illness has outlived whatever usefulness it might have had and that it now functions merely as a convenient myth. As such it is the true heir to a religious myth in general, and to the belief in witchcraft in particular; the role of these belief systems was to act as social tranquillisers, thus encouraging the hope that the mastery of certain specific problems may be achieved by means of substitutive (symbolic-magical) operations. The notion of mental illness thus serves to obscure the everyday fact that life for most people is a continuous struggle, not for biological survival, but for 'a place in the sun', 'peace of mind', or some other human value. For man aware of himself and of the world about him, once the needs for preserving the body (and perhaps the race) are more or less satisfied, the problem arises as to what he should do with himself. Sustained adherence to the myth of mental illness allows people to avoid facing this problem, believing that mental health, conceived as the absence of mental illness, automatically insures the making of right and safe choices in one's conduct of life. But the facts are all the other way. It is the making of good choices in life that others regard, retrospectively, as good mental health.

The myth of mental illness encourages us, moreover, to believe in its logical corollary: that social intercourse would be harmonious, satisfying and the secure basis of a 'good life' were it not for the disrupting influences of mental illness.

. . . Our adversaries are not demons, witches, fate, or mental illness. We have no enemy whom we can fight, exorcise, or dispel by 'cures'. What we do have are problems in living . . . mental illness is a myth, whose function it is to disguise and thus render more palatable the bitter pill of moral conflicts in human relations.

(Szasz, 1960, p. 118)

For some time after Szasz's article appeared, something of a running battle raged. Criticism was met with counter-criticism and defence with further attack. Thus, while Ausubel (1961) urged that 'it is both unnecessary and potentially dangerous to discard the concept of mental illness' (p. 74) and Macklin (1972) concluded 'that there is no compelling reason to adopt Szasz's view that mental illness is a myth and that personality disorders and psychological problems are inappropriately viewed as illness and properly to be construed as "problems in living"' (p. 363), Albee (1968) wrote that the idea that 'people who exhibit disturbed and disturbing behaviour are sick is a fundamental conceptual error' (p. 168) for which, as he later wrote, 'there is precious little evidence' (Albee, 1969, p. 872).

The medically oriented establishment has remained resistant, to some extent, to arguments against the underlying medical model and the type of intervention it provides, but in recent years things have changed radically and a number of models for conceptualising problems in social and emotional development have been developed as alternatives to the medical model. At first glance these different approaches may appear contradictory, but this is not necessarily the case and it is possible to draw from one or more of them in formulating a response which is appropriate to the difficulties which are presented and the situation in which they are to be addressed.

Behaviourism

In recent years behaviourism has tended to dominate attempts to understand and deal with emotional and behavioural difficulties in educational contexts. The ways in which behaviourism can be put into practice vary considerably (see, e.g., Wheldall, 1987) but the fundamental principles are simple. The key concept is the notion that all behaviour, including unacceptable behaviour, occurs because it is reinforced. Thus, in relation to a behavioural difficulty in school, it is necessary to examine the classroom environment and the behaviour of the teachers and other pupils, to determine how that behaviour is being reinforced. This is never easy, and the suggestion that teachers may reinforce unacceptable behaviour patterns is one that many teachers find difficult to accept. Yet teachers, even those in special schools and units, spend a large proportion of their time dealing with misbehaviour and a relatively small proportion of their time focusing on good behaviour. While the 'dealing with bad behaviour' might be done unpleasantly, with the intention of stopping it, or tolerantly, in order to communicate an understanding of the child's distress, the attention gained during these interactions can be reinforcing and, paradoxically, strengthen the very behaviour that it is intended to eliminate. Implicit in this position is the assertion that it is possible to change behaviour by manipulating the consequences of the behaviour or changing the situation in which it occurs.

Systemic approaches

The notion that behaviour is most fruitfully understood in the context of the situation in which it occurs has been developed more fully by systemic theorists (see Chapter 6). As noted above, recent research has suggested that pupil behaviour is often a function of teacher behaviour, and that if teachers wish to change the behaviour of their pupils they need to consider whether it is in any way a product of the environment which exists in the classroom and school and may have to look hard at their own behaviour. It is also the case that pupils and teachers do not come to school devoid of emotional experiences or without established patterns of behaviour; how pupils and teachers behave in school and interact with one another will inevitably reflect those experiences and response patterns. The interactive nature of behavioural patterns is recognised in behavioural theory but distinct 'systemic' theories (see Cooper and Upton, 1990a) have been advanced which seek to understand behaviour problems in schools in terms of the interactions of the persons involved, either within the school situation or in related contexts such as the family of the pupil concerned, the staff group, etc.

Within this framework, problem behaviour is not seen as originating from within pupils but from within the interaction between pupils and teachers From the ecosystemic perspective, both pupils and teachers have a rational basis for behaving in the way they do but are often locked in a circular chain of increasingly negative interaction from which neither can readily escape – the more pupils misbehave, the more negative teachers become, the more negative they become, the more pupils misbehave. The circular nature of interactional patterns of this

25

kind means that it is not appropriate to think of them in cause–effect terms; but each can be seen, and indeed is seen by the different parties, as the cause of the other. Whether we *blame* the pupils or their teachers depends on where we decide to *punctuate* the chain of events. It follows from this, that intervention can be effectively achieved at any point in the system. If the pattern is circular the circle can be broken at any point and a change in the pupils' behaviour will necessitate change in their teacher's behaviour and vice versa. As noted above in relation to the behavioural approach, such thinking is not necessarily easy for teachers to accept; recognising one's contribution to a problem situation is never comfortable.

The growing influence of the behaviourist and ecosystemic approaches can be seen as a rejection of the medical model, in that they assume a very different conceptualisation of behaviour problems.

CONTINUITY AND CHANGE

In the study of child development in general, but in the study of emotional and behavioural problems in particular, there has also been an emphasis on what has been described as the overriding importance of the early years. Thus Hurlock (1953, p. 7) wrote that:

> Childhood is the foundation period of life. This is the time when attitudes, habits and patterns of behaviour are established and when the personality is moulded. What form these will take will determine, to a large extent, how successfully or unsuccessfully the individual will be able to adjust to life as he grows older.

Assumptions about the importance of the early years and the subsequent stability of human behaviour are also particularly common in literature concerned with children's behaviour problems. Laslett (1977), for instance, defined maladjusted children as children 'whose difficulties will persist unless help is given' (p. 3) while a common complaint of special school teachers is that secondary school age referral of children reduces the possibility of success with pupils whose disturbance has been reinforced over a period of years. It is assumed that a child who displays problems during adolescence must have displayed those problems at an earlier age.

Such assumptions about the development of behaviour problems might be seen to reflect medical concepts of development paralleling those of most other aspects of child growth and development. Some thirty years ago, Stevenson questioned 'the belief that human personality is more plastic in infancy and childhood than in later years' (Stevenson, 1957, p. 152), but in 1957 Stevenson spoke, in large measure, as a lone voice. Since then, calls for a re-evaluation of the importance of the early years have increased dramatically, and a powerful lobby has developed of people who suggest that previously we may have tended to overestimate the importance of the early years and underestimate the human being's capacity for later change and development. Evidence from research (a review of which is provided by Upton, 1981) certainly suggests some continuity and consistency in behaviour, but equally it underlines the importance of variability and change. While it is apparent that a proportion of children display chronic, long-lasting behaviour problems, this group of children is small and, for the majority of children, behaviour problems appear to represent no more than a phase in development. Thus the child who is seen as a severe problem in the comprehensive school may, or may not, have experienced similar difficulties in junior school and vice versa.

Such considerations have obvious implications for dealing with behaviour problems. In particular, the concept of early intervention is rendered somewhat suspect, for implicit in this concept is the assumption that behaviour problems are long-term problems. If that small group of children for whom behaviour problems represent intractable difficulties could be identified early, intervention could be beneficial. However, at the moment there appears to be no clear way of distinguishing such children from those for whom behaviour problems represent a passing phase. While, in retrospect, from the vantage point of the secondary school, it is often easy to see continuity and clear evidence of earlier problems in an individual case, to predict which children from the many who show problems in the early school years will continue to display such problems is not possible.

CONCLUSION

In this chapter an attempt has been made to provide an overview of some key issues related to the nature and development of behaviour problems. It is clear that recent changes in the understanding of behaviour problems have shifted the locus of responsibility for the bulk of such problems away from the traditional therapeutic disciplines and moved it more directly into the community in general and schools in particular. Once behaviour problems are viewed more in terms of problems in living than as disease entities, then such problems can be seen as the responsibility of those concerned with the general socialising process. Recent evidence on the extent to which schools do influence behaviour patterns would seem to emphasise the potential importance of the school's role in dealing with behaviour problems. This is not to say that some children do not experience severe and deep-seated emotional problems that require specialist help. However, the number of children who fall into this category is relatively small and most of the behaviour problems experienced in the ordinary school would seem to be more appropriately dealt with within the situation in which they have arisen.

If such a reorientation is accepted then it would seem that much rethinking has to be done – a seemingly minor issue such as the terms that are used to describe such problems is of not inconsiderable importance as words do reflect, and affect, the way people think about problems and, more importantly, the action that is taken in response to them. Furthermore, thus far, the bulk of the literature, research, assessment techniques and treatment ideas concerning children's behaviour problems, has originated from within what might be termed the traditional therapeutic and associated academic community – i.e. psychiatrists, psychologists, sociologists and social workers. Even now, much of the interest in the importance of the school in the development of behaviour problems is coming from the same sources. It would seem vital that teachers should begin to take a greater interest in this area, and begin to examine their own institutions from their own vantage point. Teachers, in turn, tend to be dismissive of the contribution that other disciplines make, and to criticise their lack of awareness of what schools are really like and just how behaviour patterns do develop within the context of the school environment and interfere with its functioning. Suggestions for intervention are similarly frequently dismissed out of hand by teachers as impractical. If a broad conceptualisation of behaviour problems in schools is to be developed, schools must begin to take a more active role in trying to understand behaviour problems and to develop, or adapt, intervention approaches that are compatible with the ethos of schools.

2

EDUCATIONAL RESPONSES TO EMOTIONAL AND BEHAVIOURAL DIFFICULTIES

A review of changes in educational responses to emotional and behavioural difficulties can most usefully start with consideration of how schools and units for pupils with emotional and behaviour difficulties or 'maladjusted children', as they were categorised until the 1981 Education Act, have reflected different perceptual models. Laslett (1983), in a study of changing perceptions of maladjustment, notes a shift from medical to psychological and educational models. These changing perceptions have shifted the focus of concern from the personal problems of the individual pupil to the nature of the school system, and how its management may create rather than ameliorate difficulties in learning and behaviour.

Laslett's study starts from the response of teachers to the appearance of 'maladjustment' as a category of handicap in the regulations produced in 1945 to implement the intentions for providing 'special educational treatment' outlined in the 1944 Education Act. In these regulations maladjusted children were deemed to be those who 'show evidence of emotional instability or psychological disturbance and require special educational treatment in order to effect their personal, social or educational readjustment' (Laslett, 1983, p. 2).

To whom were teachers to turn for help in deciding what sort of educational process might bring about such readjustment? Who would tell them what constituted evidence of emotional instability or psychological disturbance, themselves terms as much in need of definition as maladjustment itself? Perhaps by analogy with provision for pupils with sensory and physical disabilities, where special education was often linked to hospital

31

provision, perhaps influenced by the psychoanalytic orientation of the early pioneer workers with disturbed pupils, teachers turned for help to psychiatrists. This resulted in the adoption of the medical perspective which, for many years, strongly influenced educational responses to maladjustment and to other children whose behaviour presented problems to their teachers. Disturbed behaviour was seen as resulting from some underlying condition or 'illness', and treatment was provided by therapy which emphasised paying attention to personal and social readjustment before educational difficulties.

Provision was made through Child Guidance Clinics, which served as it were as the out-patients' departments of the medical model, with special schools acting as something like an observation ward! Without stretching the comparison too far, the role of educational psychologists in testing, the role of psychiatric social workers in counselling families and the role of teachers in providing reports on behaviour all fitted neatly with the concept of a medical team. Children would be 'ascertained' as maladjusted by the psychiatrist, their progress would be assessed regularly at case conferences presided over by the psychiatrist and, if sufficient progress were made, the decision to 'de-ascertain' and readmit to the mainstream of education would be made by the psychiatrist.

THE MEDICAL MODEL

In 1955, the year in which the Underwood Committee reported on provision for maladjusted children (Ministry of Education, 1955), there were only three dozen state schools for maladjusted children, all but three of which were residential. The theoretical base for work in such schools was very much influenced by the child-centred approach associated with 'progressive' schools such as Neill's Summerhill, with its emphasis on individual freedom of expression. As Laslett (1983) points out, practice in early special schools for maladjusted children, and advice available from books about them by authors such as Wills, Winnicott, Shaw, Lennhoff and Dockar-Drysdale, drew on psychotherapeutic and social rehabilitation with little attention to classroom experience other than as source material for case histories. Problem behaviour was seen as the result of poor early care and deprivation of affection, so treatment aimed at building relationships which restored emotional growth. A further influence was the psychoanalytic perspective that repressed feelings should be brought to the surface so that insight can be gained. Together, these views provided a rationale for schools to be places of unconditional acceptance and almost boundless tolerance of even severely disturbed behaviour.

This view of the special school as a setting for clinical observation may also have owed something to an extension of the concept of 'play therapy' from the Child Guidance Clinic to the classroom. For children not yet articulate enough to participate in classic analysis, play could be used as the vehicle for enabling them to reveal their feelings. A special school might therefore be seen as a suitable place for gathering material for interpretation, with its educational function taking a very secondary role. Add to this the perception that play in itself might be therapeutic and the growth of interest in Rogerian client-centred, non-directive therapy, and it is easy to discern the reasons for the development of a style of school possibly best described as 'cathartic', encouraging the acting out of instinctual impulses and anti-social behaviour.

Although stating quite firmly that maladjustment 'is not a medical term diagnosing a medical condition', the Underwood Report (Ministry of Education, 1955), with its classification of symptoms into nervous, habit, behaviour, organic and psychotic disorders and educational difficulties, reflected the prevailing medical perspective. The report of this committee, which investigated provision for maladjusted children, reinforced the perception that maladjustment meant that there was something wrong within the child, though the Underwood Report did emphasise that much depended on an individual's relation at a particular time to people and circumstances.

Milieu therapy

This perception was reflected in the approach of schools, which sought to resolve problem behaviours by providing a more appropriate environment or 'milieu'. If emotional and behavioural difficulties had resulted from a deprived or un-happy upbringing and inadequate socialisation, then treatment required the provision of an alternative form of care which would give opportunities for building or rebuilding healthy relationships.

Wilson and Evans (1980) discerned different patterns of care: the traditional or institutional care, family-type care, planned environmental therapy and shared responsibility. Though not in practice as precisely defined into distinct categories, and with considerable overlap between different approaches within particular schools, the concept of these four schools of thought is a useful way of looking at educational provision, still mainly residential, for maladjusted children as it developed during the 1950s and 1960s.

The traditional pattern of good physical standards of care linked to strict discipline and social and vocational training was typical of the approved schools for youngsters detained by order of the court for criminal offences, but it was also typical of some of the larger homes run by charitable institutions for orphans and other deprived children. The distinction between the 'criminal' and what the nineteenth-century reformer Mary Carpenter (1851) described as the 'perishing' classes had long been seen to be a fine one. The latter were 'those who have not yet fallen into actual crime, but who are almost certain from their ignorance, destitution and the circumstances in which they were growing up, to do so, if a helping hand be not extended to raise them' (Carpenter, 1851, p. 2). Efforts to extend that helping hand had included the establishment of 'industrial' as well as reformatory schools, with the intention of separating treatment for vagrants, beggars, waifs, strays and orphans from children who committed serious crime. There were some interesting attempts to develop special provision in these establishments (Smith, 1977) but by 1933 both types of institution were lumped together as schools 'approved' by the Home Office for dealing with what by then were becoming known as juvenile delinquents.

The Children Act 1969 was itself the culmination of a series of reports and White Papers which noted the blurring of the distinction between delinquency and deprivation and sought to replace the legalistic orientation of criminal proceedings with more welfare-oriented care proceedings in the juvenile courts. The term 'approved school' was replaced by 'community home' by the 1969 Act and this gave official impetus to a move away from institutional discipline towards the second pattern described by Wilson and Evans (1980) as 'family-type care'.

Healthy growth and development depends not only on adequate food and shelter but also on the stable, continuous, dependable and loving relationship usually found within the family (Kellmer Pringle, 1974). Where this has been lacking or where it is no longer available, a residential school can aim to provide a substitute which offers predictable expectations and consistent discipline. Like a family, the school accepts that behaviour of all its members will not always be perfect, and though not condoning bad behaviour the school accepts and understands it. The school provides a reassuringly stable pattern to life, adults whose behaviour is reliable and supportive and limits which promise security and protection (Laslett, 1977). Within this pattern of nurture, there are many opportunities for teachers and care staff to give close personal attention to individuals in both classroom and social situations with chances to offer insight and support.

A more systematic approach is associated with the work of the Planned Environment Therapy Trust and is described by Righton (1975) as involving the deliberate use of everyday living experiences, shared by professional workers and clients, to find solutions to problems. Redl (1971) illustrates how this can work with children and coins the term 'life space interview' to describe how adults can use everyday incidents for the 'clinical exploitation of life events' and for 'emotional first aid on the spot' (see Chapter 3). In settling disputes and soothing temper tantrums, lessons about cause and effect can be conveyed and reassurance about continuing concern and affection can be given.

Other versions of planned environmental therapy were less interventionist, drawing more upon the notions of 'unconditional affection' and 'symptom tolerance' described in the Underwood Report and derived from the ideas of pioneer workers with maladjusted children which often combined with responsibility for management and treatment shared between staff and residents in the community (Bridgeland, 1971). Participation in decision making through some element of self-government was intended to give children practical experience of the need for rules and co-operation in daily living. Involvement might be through a formal school council or regular meetings of the whole school, or as part of a 'court' for dealing with damage, theft, bullying or other transgressions of school rules.

Even where such emphasis on self-regulation was evident, milieu therapy nonetheless continued to reflect the 'medical model' of maladjustment, which was further strengthened by the use of the description 'psychiatric disorder' for children examined for emotional and behaviour problems in a survey of the education, health and behaviour of all children in the Isle of Wight during the late 1960s. Graham and Rutter (1970) were at pains to emphasise the point that to describe children as having a psychiatric disorder did not necessarily mean they had a disease or illness, and that the description carried no connotation that treatment would necessarily benefit a child nor that psychiatrists were necessarily the best therapists for these children. However, the findings of this part of the survey refer to the proportion of children with 'clinically significant' symptoms and recommendations for treatment conclude with a complaint about the shortage of well-trained child psychiatrists and the need for better training in this area for paediatricians and general practitioners. With this background, it is not surprising that whilst 'maladjustment' was in effect merely an umbrella term administratively convenient for making special provision for certain children, schools for such children should display an emphasis on their therapeutic rather than their educational qualities.

A change of emphasis

A decade after the Isle of Wight survey, with its emphasis on 'psychiatric disorder', Wilson and Evans (1980) reported the findings of a Schools Council enquiry into the theory and practice of educational work with disturbed children. This study was concerned not only with children formally deemed maladjusted, but all those whose disruptive behaviour hampered their educational progress. It noted 'signs of a recent change in emphasis on education' (p. 40), and an increased awareness of the association between low attainment and maladjustment. In addition to its own research, the Schools Council study quoted American work which compared psycho-educational with psychodynamic approaches and showed that pupils preferred the former and that teacher–pupil relationships 'were said to be better in these classes than in those adopting the psychiatric/dynamic approach where relationships were considered more important than academic attainments' (Wilson and Evans, 1980, p. 40).

This change in emphasis may well have owed a great deal to the growth of interest in behavioural psychology with its insistence that since behaviour is learned, teachers are as well-equipped as other professionals to help disturbed children learn new and more appropriate behaviour. The inclusion within the educational service of children with severe learning difficulties, previously written off as incapable or unsuitable for education, which took place after the 1970 Education Act, also raised the profile of behavioural psychology not only in terms of behaviour modification but also in approaches to curriculum development based on task analysis of learning objectives into small, finely graded steps. Methods used successfully with children with complex learning difficulties were obviously of interest to other colleagues dealing with pupils who were difficult to teach, and the language and techniques of learning theory were familiar to most teachers.

Such developments further focused attention on the classroom rather than the clinic as the setting for intervention and this view had been supported by changes in the official procedures for the identification and assessment of pupils with special educational needs. The Department of Education and Science Circular 2/75 made it clear that, though medical opinion had still a part to play, decisions about special education were 'primarily an educational matter rather than a medical one' and considered it more appropriate that 'an experienced educational psychologist or adviser in special education should . . . assume responsibility for conveying to the authority a recommendation about the nature of special education required and where it should be provided' (DES, 1975, para. 17). Though addressing these issues with regard to special educational needs in general, the particular effect of the circular in the field of maladjustment was that, as Laslett (1983, p. 26) puts it, 'the influence of the psychiatrist waned; the status of the psychologist and the educational adviser was enhanced'.

The Warnock Report (DES, 1978) was another influence in favour of a more psycho-educational approach suggesting: 'In our view psychologists, working where necessary with psychiatrists and social workers, should remain foremost in helping teachers to deal with emotional and behavioural problems, when they occur in school ' (DES, 1978, 14: 8).

It is perhaps the insertion of 'where necessary' which most eloquently signifies the changed perception of this committee of enquiry into the education of handicapped children and young people. When the views of the committee were translated into legislation, albeit in somewhat modified form, in the Education Act 1981 and its attendant circulars on implementation, maladjusted children were no longer defined as a separate category and, in common with other pupils with special educational needs, assessment was to be based on a range of educational, psychological and medical reports. Such reports were to focus on 'learning difficulties' and the facilities and resources required to meet them. This emphasis reflected the advance of what can best be described as a 'psycho-educational' model.

CURRICULUM DEVELOPMENT

In theory, special schools for pupils with emotional and behavioural difficulties reflected these changes in emphasis in the ways in which they planned and delivered the curriculum with a perception that education in itself has a therapeutic function. Whilst there was little attention given to classroom activities in the accounts of early work with maladjusted children, Laslett (1977) and Wilson and Evans (1980) give considerable attention to the value of teaching and learning in helping children grow in confidence and self-esteem. As Laslett argues: 'What children learn and how they learn it is one of the factors in their school experience, so the curriculum should be planned to contribute as much as possible to the changes which lead to the children's adjustment' (p. 123).

Areas of the curriculum which can provide such help are physical education, drama, music, art and craft. Physical education helps increase awareness of self through its concentration on bodily strength, fitness and co-ordination. Games, as part of this area of the curriculum, should provide practice in co-operation and sharing as well as outlets for energy and aggression. Drama, like imaginative play, is an occasion for releasing feelings and discussing and interpreting them. Music offers help in understanding changes of mood and the pleasure of creativity in making one's own music. Art and craft activities help provide alternative means for communication, distraction and relaxation from other tensions and the success which comes from overcoming frustration in surmounting difficulties and producing a finished product.

In practice, Wilson and Evans found that, though they saw a great deal of remedial work on basic educational skills, and plenty of success derived from art and light craft work in the schools they visited, the use of other media to help insight and understanding was not very evident. They suggest that lack of specialist staff might be the reason why the curriculum of special schools was limited in those very areas where they might have been expected to offer more than ordinary schools.

After the 1981 Education Act, because categorical definition of special needs was no longer available, information about pupils was collated on the basis of curricular need. The advent of the National Curriculum as, at least nominally, an entitlement for all, has ended this practice, but Smith (1990) argues that these terms can still usefully distinguish the different forms of provision appropriate for dealing with emotional and behavioural difficulties of various levels of severity.

1 'Mainstream plus support' aptly describes the situation where, given additional help, individuals can cope with the normal school curriculum. This support can take the form of specialist remedial teaching and extra help in the classroom with additional resources and advice on differentiating teaching methods and materials to match individual levels of ability.

2 'Modified curriculum' describes the type of therapeutic curriculum outlined above, not widely different from the mainstream but adapted to meet different priorities, for

example, spending more time on the more therapeutic elements of the curriculum noted above.

3 'Developmental curriculum' describes provision for pupils with severe learning difficulties but can equally apply to dealing with situations where behaviour is so profoundly disturbed that a completely different perspective on curriculum planning is necessary.

Where 'mainstream plus support' is concerned, Smith (1992b) suggests that providing the full range of subjects required by the National Curriculum may squeeze out some of the imaginative, social and vocational curricular alternatives offered in the past as a means of retaining the interest and enthusiasm of older pupils, whose lack of academic progress might otherwise lead to disaffection. On the other hand, it can be argued that following an 'alternative' or 'modified' curriculum may merely signal to some pupils that they have been 'written off' by the school and that developing a 'curriculum for all' will inspire schools to think more positively about the potential of all their pupils. Smith argues that the answer lies in the ability of mainstream schools to prevent learning difficulties from becoming behavioural difficulties, as they often do, when pupils ward off feelings of inadequacy and incompetence by indulging in misbehaviour. He borrows a phrase from Hargreaves (1967) and urges schools to avoid such pupil disaffection by 'keeping them clever'. This can be achieved through curriculum planning, which develops courses matched to the ability and interests of pupils with a wide range of abilities and through other aspects of school organisation and management, which develop a sense of the school as a community, which appreciates and values all its members.

Where special schools are concerned, there is also a need to take account of the National Curriculum, particularly with regard to intentions of returning pupils to the mainstream. It is likely, however, that their distinctive feature will continue to be a more flexible and individualised approach to the curricular needs of pupils for whom the mainstream system has not proved effective. Whether described officially as 'modified' or 'developmental', the different nature and quality of learning experiences on offer should be their defence against the criticism that special schools and units for pupils with emotional and behavioural difficulties are no more than dumping grounds for children rejected by the mainstream, a criticism of special education strongly voiced by sociologists.

Special units

Tomlinson (1982) questioned what she described as the rhetoric of 'special needs' and asked whether it was anything more than a convenient means of 'legitimating the exclusion of certain children, particularly those from the "social problem class", into a separate sub-system'. Having reviewed the progress of pupils in special schools and units, Galloway and Goodwin (1987, p. 63) concluded that the evidence suggested 'that most existing special schools and units for children with behaviour problems might realistically be seen as part of the problem rather than as part of the solution'. Indeed they argued that: 'Those with adjustment difficulties may be contained in special schools and centres but there is little evidence that they actually benefit' (p. 174).

Galloway and Goodwin (1987) use the term 'disturbing' to describe pupils previously referred to as 'slow learning and maladjusted' (Galloway and Goodwin, 1979), to indicate that problems do not stem from within the child but from a lack of coherent policy at national and local level, and from features of organisation, curriculum and pastoral care in mainstream schools. They are critical not only of special schools for children with emotional, behavioural or learning difficulties but also of the range of units and special classes for 'disruptive' pupils. Some of these units had originally been set up with the intention of providing a facility which avoided the stigma of special schooling but, as Lloyd-Smith (1984) demonstrates, like special schools they show a variety of responses to different theories about models of education which are appropriate for youngsters who do not easily fit into the mainstream of education.

In his survey of the growth of provision of special units for disaffected pupils, Lloyd-Smith discerns two contemporary trends which contributed to this form of development during the 1970s. On the one hand, the deschooling movement encouraged the foundation of 'free' schools to rescue pupils from the constraints of the conventional system; on the other hand, concern for 'standards' sought to relieve teachers from the demands of disciplining unruly and reluctant learners.

Thus, amongst the 'pupil rescuers', some units represented a philosophy based on a psychotherapeutic approach similar to early schools for maladjusted children, seeking, according to Lloyd-Smith, 'to heal the damaged self-concepts of children whose experience of unsatisfactory social relationships prevents them from benefiting fully from the opportunities provided by the educational system'. Other units represented a perspective drawn from radical social work, which saw the troubled child as a victim of an inappropriate and antagonistic system, from which the unit offered 'a form of alternative schooling which seeks to teach the child how to understand and survive his disadvantaged status'.

Amongst the 'teacher relief' units, Lloyd-Smith notes a strategy designed to ensure that even the most problematic pupils were educated with an emphasis on 'progress in basic elements of the curriculum', together with efforts to arouse interest in other subjects. Though there was a focus on remedial work and widening educational opportunities in some units, others might be continuing academic work for external examinations with brighter and older adolescents. An extensive review of provision for disruptive pupils by Evans (1981) suggests that there was an excessive concentration on routine remedial reading and basic arithmetic work in many units, where a narrowed curricular diet made it increasingly difficult to arrange a return to the educational mainstream for those who had 'dropped off the edge of the known world'.

Mortimore *et al.* (1983) looked at centres for truants and for disruptive pupils and saw advantages in the possibility of such arrangements allowing teachers greater freedom to experiment with innovatory methods and offering pupils a real change from schools in which they had been unsuccessful. However, practical difficulties in reintegration were encountered, because there was little relation to the mainstream in the aims, objectives, rules, expectations and ethos of the units. Another problem was that staff felt isolated, inadequately trained and overlooked in career advancement.

More recent research by Cooper, Smith and Upton (1990)

shows that the lack of opportunity for professional development and training is an experience shared by teachers in special schools for pupils with emotional and behaviour difficulties. This is not simply a matter of staff gaining the additional status that derives from attaining advanced qualifications. Specialised training enables staff to recognise and define the body of knowledge which provides the rationale for working in a particular way. It is particularly important that people working with youngsters whose behaviour is erratic and impulsive should develop a theoretical framework which helps them respond to challenging behaviour not merely by instinct but through the application of a broader treatment strategy to a specific situation. It is also essential that they should become aware of alternative approaches, so that if their normal strategy is not working they may analyse what is going wrong and perhaps try another approach. In this respect it is important to remember that it is often true to say that there is nothing more practical than a good theory!

CONCLUSION

The issues discussed in this chapter illustrate the changing nature of provision for pupils with emotional and behaviour difficulties and show how educational responses have reflected a variety of different views on the nature and development of behaviour problems. The rest of this book will explore these issues further, examining particular practical applications of different theoretical approaches in Part II and suggesting ways forward in the process of institutional change through developing whole school policies, which may erode institutional, methodological and theoretical boundaries, in Part III.

Part II

DEVISING
SOLUTIONS

OVERVIEW

In this part of the book we look at the theories which have informed and justified different approaches to the solution of problems presented by children with emotional and behavioural difficulties. The possibilities offered to teachers by theories based on dynamic psychotherapy and behavioural psychology are discussed, with particular consideration given to their application to practice in schools. The thinking behind the newer and less familiar ecosystemic approach is introduced and explained, and a conceptual framework is suggested for the apparently pragmatic business of classroom management.

Acknowledging the importance of relationships, which helps those involved understand and resolve individual distress, does not imply that problems are entirely within the individual. However, an awareness of the insights provided by psychodynamic theory can help teachers offer therapeutic counselling and guidance to pupils with severe and persistent behaviour problems. In Chapter 3 we outline the main principles of psychotherapeutic theory and show how these may be helpful to teachers. This chapter expands further on the application of the 'medical model' described in Chapter 1, which informed and directed many of the pioneer responses to the education of maladjusted children described in Chapter 2. From this perspective, it is necessary to be familiar with key elements of the psychodynamic approach, such as unconscious processes, anxiety and psychic pain, defence mechanisms, motivational drives and developmental phases, and these are explained in this chapter.

Psychodynamic theory generally relates problems in

emotional development to unfortunate experiences, usually in the early years, which interfere with normal progress through the stages of social and emotional growth. This approach, and therapeutic intervention derived from it, is exemplified through examining the work of Winnicott, Dockar-Drysdale and Wills. This chapter also considers different levels of psychotherapy, different therapeutic settings and guidelines for effective therapeutic communication, thus expanding on the concept of 'milieu' therapy introduced in Chapter 2. Whilst it may appear that the ideas introduced in Chapter 3 are most relevant to the milieu of the special school, it is argued that the demystification of psychodynamic theory can help all teachers in the process of engaging in constructive dialogue with disturbed or disturbing pupils, an idea which recurs in discussing the concept of 'mediation' introduced in Chapter 6.

Behavioural psychology played a considerable part in the change of emphasis from medical to educational models of problem behaviour noted in Chapter 2, but sometimes teachers have been resistant to what they have perceived as an overly manipulative and experimental approach more suited to the laboratory than the classroom. Chapter 4 again provides a demystification of the terminology and methodology of an approach often seen as too esoteric for everyday application in schools, and illustrates how knowledge of learning theory can be of practical utility in the classroom. This chapter looks at how the key concept stated in Chapter 1, that behaviour occurs and continues to occur because it is reinforced, can be applied by teachers in changing behaviours which are presenting problems. The chapter further deals with the steps involved in setting up a programme for behaviour modification, specifying and measuring behaviour, setting goals and arranging cues and reinforcement to encourage their attainment. Each step is discussed in terms of how this approach might be used in busy classrooms, in ways which apply theory appropriately, without embroiling teachers too much in the procedural niceties of experimental method. In particular, emphasis is placed on setting worthwhile goals, extending to social as well as academic skills, and arranging cues and reinforcers which fit naturally within the classroom environment. Evaluating the success of a behavioural approach is considered, not only in relation to achieving measurable changes in behaviour, but also in terms of the costs and benefits to the teacher of the necessary investment of time and energy in adopting this approach.

This concern with context is continued and expanded in the next chapter, which draws on knowledge from the fields of humanistic psychology and family therapy to introduce the concept of the ecosystemic approach. This view stresses the interactional nature of behaviour and the ways in which changes within one part of a system of relationships will affect other parts of the system. From a discussion of the work of different family therapists within this tradition, principles relevant to work in schools are discerned and key components of an ecosystemic approach to school behaviour problems are outlined. From this perspective, Chapter 5 shows how problem behaviour can be seen as a product of patterns of social interaction which can be analysed in simple terms of the ecosystem of the classroom, or in more complex terms of the behaviour serving wider ecosystems, such as patterns within the family. Crucially, the ecosystemic approach sees problem behaviour as part of a cyclical chain of actions and reactions within which oppositional tactics will merely exacerbate the problem, so intervention based on this approach must eschew confrontation and esteem co-operation. Possibilities for helping teachers make such interventions are discussed and a case study is used to demonstrate the applicability of this approach within the classroom.

The ecosystemic approach places considerable emphasis on the importance of teachers being aware of a variety of perspectives on a problem and Chapter 6 continues this theme, by constructing a conceptual framework linking the theory and practice of classroom management which integrates work from three separate sources, on levels of analysis of disruptive behaviour, aspects of teaching technique and teachers' beliefs on discipline.

At the first level of dealing with incidents in the classroom, *management* skills are the aspect of teaching technique deployed to prevent or avoid disruption but if it does occur, to minimise its effect on the smooth running of lessons. At the second level, teachers focus more on intervention with individuals and their personal beliefs on discipline will influence decisions about whether the aspects of teaching technique which they utilise are those of *mediation* through counselling or other less directive, more child-centred responses, or whether they move along the continuum of teacher behaviour to more directive teacher-centred techniques of *modification*. At the third level of analysis of interactions within institutions the related aspect of teaching technique is *monitoring*, here involving collegial evaluation of whole school behaviour policies.

Whilst for convenience considered in separate chapters, it is intended that the solutions devised from different perspectives should not be seen as alternatives, between which teachers must make a choice, but as a range of longer-term strategies and shorter-term tactics from which an approach may be chosen to suit a particular situation. Being aware of these different approaches, and the theories which underpin them, will also help awareness and understanding of the aims and purposes of other teachers, psychologists, medical and social workers engaged in helping children with emotional and behavioural difficulties.

3

THE IMPORTANCE OF
RELATIONSHIPS

In responding to emotional and behavioural difficulties in schools it is important, as has been argued in earlier chapters, that intervention does not focus exclusively on the pupil and ignore the role which can be played by teachers, the school and the family in the generation and maintenance of behaviour patterns. A balanced view is essential if appropriate attention is to be given to the various factors which might influence the behaviour of any individual child or young person. Yet, at the centre of all such problems is the individual, the person in whose behaviour the problems are reflected. It is thus important to consider what significance teachers and schools might appropriately place on the individual in trying to understand behaviour which they find troublesome, and to what extent intervention strategies should focus on the individual pupil.

One argument for an 'individual focus' is that behavioural problems in schools sometimes reflect the existence of deep-seated emotional difficulties. Thus, the Elton Committee of Enquiry into discipline in schools (DES, 1989a) concluded that a 'small minority of pupils have . . . severe and persistent behaviour problems as a result of emotional, psychological or neurological disturbance'. Indeed, it is this group of pupils which appears to constitute the basis of the official definition of emotional and behavioural difficulties in Britain. In Circular 23/89 (DES, 1989b) such pupils are defined as children who

exhibit unusual problems of adaptation to a range of

physical, social and personal situations. They may set up barriers between themselves and their learning environment through inappropriate, aggressive, bizarre or withdrawn behaviour. Some children will have difficulty making sense of their environment because they have a severe pervasive developmental disorder or more rarely an adult type psychosis.

[They] have developed a range of strategies for dealing with day-to-day experiences that are inappropriate and impede normal personal and social development, and make it difficult for them to learn.

(p. 3, paras 8, 10)

If the validity of this definition is accepted it is clearly important that an attempt is made to understand the 'dis-ease' which the individual is experiencing and help him or her to deal more effectively with that. In situations where the problem is clearly not one of emotional disturbance and where the problem is in no sense entirely located within the individual, the notion of helping pupils to better understand and cope with difficult situations is arguably still appropriate. To help unhappy or distressed individuals does not necessarily assume that they are to blame for the situation or that their problems are entirely of their own making.

DYNAMIC PSYCHOTHERAPY

Individual therapy and counselling are well established as ways of providing therapeutic help for individuals who are experiencing emotional difficulties and many different theories have been developed on which such intervention can be based. 'Dynamic psychotherapy' is a term used to refer to a major group of theories which share a common focus on the inner world of feelings and emotions and a belief that change occurs by helping the troubled individual to gain insight into the links between present events and previous experience.

'Scientific' formulations of psychodynamic theory and practice are relatively recent and can be traced back to the work of Freud in the first half of this century, but many of the key concepts have a long history and documented examples of psychodynamic explanations of behaviour can be found in the writings of Aristotle, Shakespeare and Rousseau. Whyte (1962) and Ellenberger (1970) provide numerous historical instances of dynamically oriented practice long before the twentieth century. In this sense, Freud did not invent psychotherapy: rather he translated long-standing assumptions about human behaviour into a scientific framework.

Theoretical background

As was noted above, the term 'dynamic psychotherapy' is a broad one which encompasses a wide variety of theories which differ in many important respects. At the same time, it is possible to see within these theories common elements which allow us to speak of them as having some underlying unity. Brown and Pedder (1979) identify five principles which they see as underlying all psychodynamic theory. These are:

1 unconscious processes;
2 anxiety and psychic pain;
3 defence mechanisms;
4 motivational drives;
5 developmental phases.

Unconscious processes

The existence of different levels of psychological functioning is a central concept in the psychodynamic approach. Freud differentiated between three levels of mental activity: conscious, pre-conscious and unconscious. The concept of conscious mental activity is self-explanatory in that it refers to any activity of which the individual is currently aware, or conscious. Pre-conscious material refers to that which is currently not in the individual's immediate awareness, but which can relatively easily be brought to the surface. Names, telephone numbers and other simple factual data are good examples of material that can easily slip into the pre-conscious level but this can also be the case with painful memories or disagreeable feelings. Unconscious material is much less readily accessible and usually involves active repression of material that is incompatible with the individual's view of self, or a potential source of too much guilt, anxiety or pain.

From the viewpoint of therapeutic intervention the level of unconscious mental activity is a key one, for in the psycho-dynamic framework it is unconscious processes that are the primary determinants of behaviour. Thus, in attempting to understand a pupil who exhibits disturbed behaviour in school it is at the level of the unconscious that we must look for the real reasons for the misbehaviour and it is the same level at which we must work in order to effect changes in the pupil's emotional state and external behaviour.

Anxiety and psychic pain

One of the reasons why emotional experiences are not assimilated into our conscious view of ourselves is the anxiety (or psychic pain) which such material may cause. Feeling unloved or unwanted by one's parents, for example, is not easy to accept. While it is possible for considerable amounts of anxiety to be tolerated, even for relatively long periods, and while a certain level of anxiety is helpful in fostering optimal performance especially in competitive situations, high levels of anxiety can produce serious emotional distress.

Recognition of this process is helpful in any attempt to understand pupils who exhibit evidence of emotional difficulties but equally important is the fact that the most common means of dealing with anxiety and psychic pain is the mobilisation of defence mechanisms.

Defence mechanisms

Defence mechanisms are ways in which we deal with aspects of ourselves which, if consciously experienced, would cause excessive anxiety or psychic pain. Common examples of defence mechanisms include:

- *Repression*: blocking off memories and feelings that are unpleasant or unacceptable at the conscious level of functioning.
- *Denial*: forgetting of unpleasant events.

- *Projection*: externalisation of unacceptable feelings and the attribution of these to others.
- *Rationalisation*: the justification of an action or re-action without any awareness of its real meaning.
- *Regression*: the reversion to an earlier, or more childlike way of behaving than that at which the child is generally functioning to obtain a desired response.
- *Displacement*: the deflection of feelings on to a person or thing other than the one that provoked them as a result of a fear of expressing them directly to that person or thing.

The variety of defence mechanisms is immense and the above represent but a small selection of these. Everyone needs, and uses, defence mechanisms and they can be vital to the individual's maintenance of emotional stability. Such mechanisms do, however, vary in the extent to which they permit healthy emotional functioning and are in the child's or young person's best interests. For example, a pupil's aggressive behaviour towards teachers may be interpreted as being more to do with feelings of anger towards his or her parents rather than anything directly related to teachers (displacement). While it may be 'safer' for the pupil to vent these feelings at school, rather than at home, it can serve to exacerbate the situation in that it is unlikely that this will be appreciated by the teachers whose negative responses may serve to heighten the feelings of rejection which gave rise to the behaviour in the first place.

Motivational drives

This is the area in which psychodynamic theorists have diverged most significantly from Freud's original thinking. Freud, as readers will probably be aware, was primarily concerned with the importance of instincts and particularly those of sexuality. Freud's theory has been a powerful explanatory force but more recent theorists have moved away from this to more broadly and socially based conceptualisations. Of particular relevance to workers with disturbed children is the work of object-relations theorists such as Winnicott (1965) and Guntrip (1971), who have emphasised the importance of the drive to seek relationships with others. Thus, rather than the early parent/child

55

relationship being described within the context of a child seeking satisfaction of an oral impulse, we have a situation described more in terms of parent and child finding emotional satisfaction through the feeding relationship. In this context it is conflict, or breakdown, in early supportive relationships that is consequently seen as the key to understanding emotional turmoil and distress.

Developmental phases

Central to most dynamic theorists is the concept of human development being characterised by developmental phases through which the individual must pass to attain a state of emotional maturity. Freud postulated a series of stages (the oral, anal, phallic, Oedipal, latency, puberty) based on psycho-sexual development. Progress through these stages depended on the satisfaction of the pleasure-seeking drive involved, whereby inadequate satisfaction at any one stage would inhibit development in successive stages and affect the final pattern of development. Thus, inadequate resolution of Oedipal or Electra complexes (involving the child 'falling in love' with the parent of the opposite sex) would affect not only the child's ability to move through the latency period and to resolve the problems of adolescence but would also affect the child's adoption of an appropriate sex role and subsequent sexual relationships.

More recently, theorists such as Erikson (1965) and Winnicott (1965) have developed similar hierarchical structures to explain developmental progress. Brown and Pedder (1979) draw on a number of these in postulating their own framework for emotional development which they conceptualise in terms of the following stages:

1 *Dependence (0–1)* The suggestion here is that in the first year of life the child gains a growing awareness of the outside world and of self as being distinct from others. Gradually, as children differentiate themselves from their mother, they become anxious about the possible loss of her. How the mother reacts to this is seen as being central to subsequent development in that it is in this process that basic trust in others is established; a trust which determines a child's

subsequent reactions to all further anxiety. Failure to establish this trust is seen as a basis for subsequent emotional disturbance.

2 *Separation/individualisation (1–3)* This stage represents a logical extension of the development of identity which was begun in the previous period and involves the establishment of, and differentiation between, dependence and independence. It is considered vital that in this process the child is able to establish a feeling of independence but at the same time maintain some feeling of dependence, belonging and attachment.

3 *Rivalry (3–5)* This involves the development of sexual identity in the child and is a process which Brown and Pedder describe in terms which are very similar to those which Freud employed in relation to the Oedipal and Electra conflicts. But, while Brown and Pedder see the process as being essentially the same as that described by Freud, they see the process in much broader terms than Freud. Consequently, they dismiss Freud's more literal interpretation of the child's jealousy of the same-sex parent and wishes to have intercourse with the opposite-sex parent and talk in less dramatic terms of the child's wish for closer relationships and of the mild rivalry to which this may give rise.

4 *Psycho-sexual moratorium (6+)* Within this context, by the age of 6, the child's basic patterns of emotional responses will have been established. Ways of integrating internal and external pressures and conflict and a range of coping strategies and defence mechanisms will have been established. Clearly, development does not stop here, but whether early crises have been resolved for good or ill, and the extent to which sufficient trust, autonomy and initiative have been developed, will determine the individual's attitude and response to subsequent life experiences.

5 *Psycho-social moratorium (adolescence)* In adolescence the individual has to work out a new psycho-social identity which to some extent repeats the early process of separation from mother which was experienced during the separation/individualisation phase. The experience of that prior process will affect this later one, but at the same time constitutes a further occasion in which to establish independence while at the same time recognising continuing dependence.

Within this process the importance of early experience is clear; patterns laid down in childhood, according to this model, are paramount and will affect behaviour in all subsequent situations. However, as was noted in the section relating to adolescence, subsequent life experiences can modify the results of prior experience. Indeed, if this were not so, therapeutic intervention would not be possible.

PROBLEMS IN SOCIAL AND EMOTIONAL DEVELOPMENT

As was noted above psychodynamic theory generally locates the origins of problems in social and emotional development in the early years of life and the quality of early relationships. Winnicott (1965), for example, accounts for emotional disturbance and behaviour problems in children in terms of a failure in the infant's environment during the critical period of dependence on mother (i.e. 0–3 years). In this context Winnicott saw such children as not having experienced a 'good enough' relationship with their mother or, as he subsequently conceded, a good enough mother substitute. (The sexist bias of psychodynamic theory is an issue that many readers may wish to take further and are referred to the works of Mitchell, 1974; Miller, 1976; Chodorow, 1978.)

Obvious examples of the influence of early experience can be seen in cases where children have been raised in care or in institutions where discontinuity and frequent change make it difficult for children to experience a relationship based on trust and continuity of experience. However, children raised in 'normal' family situations are by no means guaranteed nurturance from parents who are capable of providing such loving relationships.

Central also to Winnicott's theory are the notions of integration and non-integration. Integration refers to the individual's total acceptance of self; of all component parts and characteristics, both those that are readily acceptable and those that are not. Crucial to the development of this feeling of integration is the mother's (and/or, arguably, the father's or mother substitute's) unconditional acceptance of the child. According to Winnicott, many emotionally disturbed children experience only conditional acceptance from their parent whereby parts of the child's emerging self are not accepted unreservedly. Such aspects of self as are rejected may then be denied by the child, be displaced on to others, or expressed in unacceptable ways. Klein (1932) also explores this issue and focuses, in particular, on the role that the mother plays in helping the child to accept frustration, hostility and anger. As part of the relationship with a 'good mother' Klein sees that the child is gradually able to accept and tolerate negative aspects of self rather than disowning them or projecting them on to others.

Further, Winnicott talks specifically of the anti-social child as one who has experienced some of a good-enough relationship but then subsequently lost it; the response is primarily one of anger based on intense feelings of loss. Such children present a hopeful prognosis in Winnicott's view as they are seen as trying to get what they need from the world, to recover what they once had. Within a dynamic framework, what they need to regain their loss is a trusting relationship which will survive the demands they make upon it and the tests to which they put it. The failure of any relationship to survive these tests confirms the child's original sense of loss and distrust.

The severely withdrawn, psychotic child, on the other hand, is seen by Winnicott as a child whose relationships have failed at a very early age, usually during the first 6 months, and who has consequently never established any feeling or experienced any sense of loss and can be seen to be making no effort to recover a previously experienced good relationship.

Dockar-Drysdale (1974) has expanded on this idea and has identified three distinct groups of children whose problem she relates directly to the stage at which interruption of primary experience took place, viz: 'frozen' children; 'archipelago' children; and 'false-selves'.

- *Frozen children* she refers to as those who are the least integrated; children 'who have suffered interruption of primary experience at the point where they and their mothers would be commencing the separating out process, having been as it were broken off rather than separated out from their mothers'. She goes on to describe them as having 'survived by perpetuating a pseudo-symbiotic state; without boundaries to personality, merged with their environment, and unable to make any real object relationship, or to feel the need for them' (p. 99).

- *Archipelago children* are described by Dockar-Drysdale as those who have made some progress towards integration but not sufficient to allow them to function as integrated, whole individuals. She writes of them as being 'made up of ego islets which have never fused into a continent, a total person. For this reason we call them archipelago children' (p. 99). More specifically she describes their behaviour as being char-acterised by wild swings; from aggressive, anti-social and violent panics to being extremely gentle, quiet and totally subdued. Such children, according to Dockar-Drysdale, are easier to help than 'frozen' children in that they experience more difficulties in life because of their wild behavioural shifts. In consequence they are frequently unhappy and aware that they need help.

- *False-selves*, as the term implies, refers to those children who have built up a facade which, while it seems real enough, serves primarily to disguise the lack of a real sense of identity. In many situations the false-self serves admirably but in any in-depth relationship proves to be lacking. The child is, thus, unable to enter into any meaningful relationship.

A variation on the theme of false-self is the caretaker-self wherein a 'little self' exists but is, for most part, hidden away behind the caretaker-self. For example, the caretaker-self may be violent and aggressive, or delinquent, and thus effectively hide a more caring, thoughtful and lovable 'little self'. Such children are seen to have progressed some way towards integration but to have been stopped in this development.

More generally, dynamic therapists talk of emotional dif-ficulties in terms of inner conflict; conflict which may focus on 'dis-ease' or alienation about some aspect of self or dis-satisfaction with some aspect of relationships with others. In this context, the observed behaviour which may lead to a child being regarded as a problem must be regarded as symptoms of the distress produced by this inner conflict. To be effective, therapy must therefore focus on the resolution of the inner conflict as well as the external symptoms expressed in behaviour.

THE THERAPEUTIC PROCESS

It is unfortunate that to many people, especially teachers, dynamic psychotherapy is seen as a highly specialised and somewhat esoteric approach, the use of which must be reserved to those workers who have received appropriately specialised training or who work under the direction of such a person. To some extent such a reaction is not surprising. Psychoanalysis, for example, requires extensive training which usually assumes that the therapist will have undergone his or her own analysis and which consequently often involves a period of several years. Traditionally, such an approach has involved individual therapy carried out extensively (usually on a daily basis) and over an extended period of time.

Classic accounts of such work with children have been provided by Klein (1961), Axline (1964) and Winnicott (1977). These make for fascinating reading and they are strongly recommended to any reader who is not familiar with them; they provide an insight into dynamic psychotherapy in its pure form. All draw our attention to the depth of relationship required between therapist and child and highlight the special skills required by the therapist to function in this way.

Similarly, much pioneer work in the education of 'maladjusted' children grew out of this sort of clinical work and advocated the need for a highly specialised environment; a therapeutic community wherein the principles of traditional analysis could still be applied. Dockar-Drysdale (1974), for example, clearly has such a community in mind when she writes about the provision of primary experience in a special school in relation to the three groups of children described above: frozen children, archipelago children and false-selves.

Frozen children, she says, must be provided with emotional experiences which will enable them to separate out; to establish an identity and to recognise boundaries between self and others. With archipelago children therapy must focus on fostering greater integration, and involve a breakdown of defences and progress through complete dependence on the therapist. With false- and caretaker-self children, therapy depends upon helping the child 'to regress to the point where development originally came to a standstill, often reaching a state of psychic fusion with

61

the therapists, from which they can advance to a more adequate integration as a whole people' (p. 101). Most importantly, Dockar-Drysdale describes in some depth and in very practical terms, how such goals may be achieved. Furthermore, her own work, and the work of her successors at the Mulberry Bush School, provides eloquent testimony to the fact that these ideas can be translated into good practice, given sufficient staff training and support.

However, to many teachers, including those with special training and/or experience as teachers of children with emotional and behavioural difficulties, these suggestions appear highly sophisticated and, as a result, in the author's experience at least, they are frequently either rejected out of hand or described as 'fascinating but not practical in my situation'. As a result few recent examples can be found in the literature of the use of these ideas either in special or ordinary schools although, as Reeves (1983) makes clear in describing current practice in the Mulberry Bush School, such ideas are still practicable even within a much changed context of special educational provision to that which pertained when Dockar-Drysdale was involved in its establishment. Indeed, the esoteric nature of the suggestions may be one factor in accounting for the recent popularity of behaviour modification techniques, especially amongst those teachers working in other than residential schools. Yet there is much within this framework that has relevance for all teachers and which can be used to enhance the quality of teacher–pupil relationships and render them more rather than less therapeutic.

Levels of psychotherapy

In trying to understand the potential value of ideas derived from dynamic psychotherapy for teachers and schools it is important to recognise that the approach can be seen in a much broader context than is implied in the more specialised examples of its application as are cited above. The essential nature of dynamic psychotherapy is captured by Brown and Pedder (1979, p. ix) when they write that psychotherapy 'is essentially a conversation which involves listening to and talking with those in trouble with the aim of helping them to understand and resolve their predicament'.

This clearly suggests the possibility of therapy taking place on levels other than that of in-depth analysis. Indeed, if we conceive of psychotherapy as Brown and Pedder do in this quotation, then we are talking of a process which can occur at many levels. Some of these are clearly highly sophisticated in that they involve dialogue between a person in distress and another who has specialist training which enables him or her to use that dialogue to maximum effect. However, such dialogue can take place at an informal level, between friends, colleagues and relations with people who may have no professional training in psychotherapy. The value of talking problems through, of simply listening to someone in distress, of sharing grief, are things that are widely regarded as important features of good relationships.

This concept of different levels of psychotherapy has been formalised by Brown and Pedder who talk of outer, intermediate

Figure 1 Levels of psychotherapy

A. OUTER (support and counselling)	1	Unburdening of problems to a sympathetic listener.
	2	Ventilation of feelings within a supportive relationship.
	3	Discussion of current problems with a non-judgemental helper.
B. INTERMEDIATE	4	Clarification of problems, their nature and origins, within a deepening relationship.
	5	Confrontation of defences.
	6	Interpretation of unconscious motives and transference phenomena.
C. DEEPER (exploration and analysis)	7	Repetition, remembering and reconstruction of the past.
	8	Regression to less adult and less irrational functioning.
	9	Resolution of conflicts by re-experiencing and working them through.

Source: Brown and Pedder, (1979, p. 95)

and deeper psychotherapy and within these three levels, of nine stages of therapeutic activity (see Figure 1). Effective interaction at the deeper, and the upper end of the intermediate level (stage 5 and above) clearly requires a high degree of specialist skill. Indeed, the depth at which one would be working is such that people other than those with special training should not even attempt to engage in therapy at these levels. On the other hand therapeutic interactions at the outer, and lower end of the intermediate levels (stage 4 and below) are ones into which any teacher, or member of child care staff in the case of special schools, should be capable of entering with good effect.

The therapeutic relationship

The key to dynamic psychotherapy, at whatever level one is operating, is the quality of the relationship that exists between the therapist and the client. Above all it must be one of trust, in which the client feels able to engage in honest and direct communication and which will gradually lead to a greater acceptance of self and a growing understanding of the nature of underlying disease and distress. Obviously such a relationship is not one that can be instantly created and in many schools is one against which a number of features of school life militate. For example, the teacher's role as classroom disciplinarian, administrator of school rules, and creator of an effective learning environment does not always sit easily with that of the under-standing and empathic listener. Implicit in this concept of therapeutic relationship is the notion of being on the pupil's side and of conveying to the pupil something of the feeling of unconditional acceptance that was referred to above as an essential component of 'good-enough mothering'. Hopefully, as the pupil establishes a growing sense of trust in the relationship he or she will experience an increasing sense of acceptance of both self and others and, through verbalisation of thoughts and feelings, come to gain insight into aspects of self or of relation-ships which were previously not understood but which have been a continuing source of unhappiness and distress.

The therapeutic setting

Establishing a therapeutic relationship of the kind described above depends in no small measure on the existence of a conducive environment, the smallest features of which must be seen to be in sympathy with that relationship. A conducive environment can, perhaps, be most easily established in the context of a special individual counselling situation. Here, the teacher can control the total environment and ensure that everything that happens in that room is consonant with the therapeutic aims of the session. On a broader front, a single class can provide a similar environment irrespective of the way in which the rest of the school functions. Many adjustment units or classes function in this way to provide a sanctuary in which such therapeutic relationships may be created. Ideally, however, the total school environment should be sensitive to the emotional needs of pupils. It is possible, as was noted above in relation to pioneer work in the field of maladjustment, for schools to function as therapeutic communities but this is probably only realistic in relation to special schools. Nonetheless, ordinary schools can be organised in ways which maximise their therapeutic potential.

One of the most readable accounts of how a school might function as a therapeutic community is provided by Wills (1960). If a special school is going to serve therapeutic as well as educational aims, Wills argued that the school should be characterised by three features as perceived by the child:

1 It is mine.
2 It is permanent.
3 It is safe.

It is mine

It is vital according to Wills that we must convey to pupils the idea that the school belongs to them, not to the teachers, or the Local Education Authority or the Board of Governors. To this end, he suggests, that the life of the school should revolve around the pupils. Thus, pupils must matter more than furniture and adults' time should be no more important than that of the pupils. More significantly, he argued that schools should be run democratically with children sharing the responsibility for decisions about day-to-day routine and larger issues in which they can legally and realistically be involved.

It is permanent

In relation to special schools for 'maladjusted' children, Wills argued that they should try to provide children with something of a sense of permanency which they may not have experienced previously in their own homes (or school careers). In this context, he suggests that these children should experience as few staff changes as possible, particularly where these are occasioned by internal school organisation (e.g. timetabling). He also argues on a broader scale for stability in school placement and as few 'between-school' changes as possible. In particular, he stresses the need for follow-up, whereby a member of the school staff functions as a link person with the child once he or she moves on from the special placement.

It is safe

Wills argues that a prime function of any special provision must be to provide a refuge for the child from the troubles of the outside world. To set down rules for the creation of such a sanctuary, he says, is difficult, but notes the following:

1 adults should be consistently warm and affectionate;
2 an adult who is charged with trying to establish a therapeutic relationship with a child should not also be involved with administering punishment;
3 punishment may, however, have a part to play in an established relationship where it can be administered in the broader context of a loving relationship;
4 there should be shared responsibility;
5 to counter the possibility of chaos in a non-punitive, self-governing institution there should be clearly established routines and regulations; e.g. set timetables, and clear rules and regulations;
6 in residential schools staff rotas should be regular and as unchanging as possible.

More generally, Wills talks about the importance of *loving and giving*. He argues strongly that staff must be willing to enter into a 'loving' relationship with the children but stresses one cannot do therapeutic work on the basis of unbridled feelings. Rather, he talks of the need to recognise, control and guide feelings. He admits that not all children are instantly lovable and that staff will not always feel an emotional drive to love all their charges. He suggests that, initially, staff may have to force themselves to like some children, but notes how such feelings can soon become real. On a practical level he stresses:

1 The importance of initial greetings – these he argues are crucial to the child's perceptions of atmosphere and can determine the child's long-term response.
2 The importance of an informal atmosphere, including the use of first names and nicknames.
3 The need for permission to be given to the children to experiment with relationships and to be allowed to choose the adult(s) with whom they wish to relate.
4 The ability of staff to recognise children's advances for what they are – e.g. that aggression can be an attempt to suppress a growing positive feeling.
5 The need for school organisation to allow adults to spend time with individuals, even if, for example, the child is in a different teaching group.
6 The need for staff to be able to cope with a number of such relationships. He notes that the demands which such competitive relationships may impose can be difficult to cope with, but equates this with the parent's role in relating with siblings.
7 The importance of recognising that some staff may be more popular than others in the extent to which they are sought out by children (and of the need to sometimes support staff in relation to this).
8 The fact that such work is emotionally exhausting.

Wills also places a considerable emphasis on the importance of tolerance. He advocates that a special school should be both tolerant and permissive for the following reasons:

1 Such an atmosphere is an ideal environment in which the child can come to learn what is important/unimportant in the views of others.
2 It is only in such an atmosphere that it is possible to really get to know a child.
3 Such an atmosphere encourages a child to display relevant symptoms.
4 It facilitates the integration of new children with whom we can only gradually run the risk of correcting, or imposing limits on, their behaviour.

At the same time he stresses that children should not be protected from the consequences of their actions; rather they should be helped to face them with the support of a loving and caring relationship.

Wills was writing over thirty years ago and while some of his ideas may seem utopian it is interesting to note one of the conclusions of the Elton Report (DES, 1989a) in which it is stated that 'the most effective schools seem to be those that have created a positive atmosphere based on a sense of community and shared values' (p. 13) and how closely his ideas equate with those which are discussed in Chapter 5 as having been identified more recently as characterising effective schools.

Therapeutic communication

Given an appropriate environment, the dialogue that takes place between teacher and pupil is vital to the success of any therapeutic aims the teacher may have. In schools, in contrast to clinics or individual counselling, teachers only rarely have the luxury of engaging in extended and uninterrupted discourse with individual pupils. They do, however, have frequent opportunities in the course of normal school activities and general teacher–pupil interaction to take advantage of situations in which pupils can be particularly responsive to offers of help and support: e.g. after an emotional outburst, or during a period of apparent distress, or simply during a quiet moment. Such situations require great skill on the part of the teacher, for responses usually need to be spontaneous with little time to plan or structure the intervention. But situations such as those listed above provide excellent opportunities to express acceptance of pupils, to listen and to ask questions that lead children to a deeper insight of themselves and their actions. For these occasions a set of practicable guide-lines, called the 'life space interview', can provide a helpful framework for teachers to work within.

Redl (1966) defined the 'life space interview' as referring 'to those cases in which the adults find it necessary to surround a youngster's experience at a given time with some form of verbal communication that has the purpose of regulating the impact of this experience on the child' (p. 39). By implication it is a technique that can be used appropriately in any situation; the classroom, playground, corridor or office are all situations in which it may be suitable to undertake a life space interview.

According to Redl (1966) the life space interview can be used for two main purposes: emotional first aid and the clinical exploitation of life events. The first may be relevant in any crisis situation when the aim is to help the child recover from an upsetting or distressing incident but where constraints of time or place or the child's needs may dictate that nothing more intensive is desirable or possible. The second is more relevant at times when it seems that some longer-term gains may be accrued by the child from a more in-depth exploration of the issue. In either case, however, it is suggested that the most advantageous point at which to start such a dialogue is an immediate incident, with a problem which has arisen spontaneously rather than one which is raised formally in a counselling setting. Clearly, not all situations lend themselves to such exploration and care has to be taken to ensure that the issue that is identified for a life space interview is, in fact, appropriate – e.g. a potential disciplinary problem is unlikely to be suitable.

Specific guidelines for carrying out a life space interview have been provided by a number of authors. Morse (1969, pp. 127–8) listed the following suggestions:

1 Make certain, in a non-judgemental and non-threatening way, that the perception of the pupil is clearly expressed by him [sic] and on his own terms, distorted though this may seem. Avoid trying to discover legal truth or who did what first and so on.

2 Test for depth and spread of behaviour – are there other related problems and is this really the central issue? Attempt to determine how this is related to the pupil's personality.

3 Try to discover how the pupil's value system relates to this problem – ask the question 'Well what do you think ought to be done about this?'

4 Highlight reality factors in the school milieu which have implications if the behavior continues.

5 Explore the pupil's motivation for change – i.e. how he thinks he might be helped, and what role the teacher might have in supporting reasonable subsequent management of the behavior in question.

6 Develop a follow through plan with the pupil – this must be realistic and relevant and incorporate an awareness of the school's resources, its willingness to act, and its escape hatches.

Such steps provide a useful framework for staff to follow and which can help to make even everyday interactions with children more therapeutic. Further references to the use of life space interviews can be found in Dupont (1969) and Gobell (1980). More detailed suggestions for the development and use of psychotherapeutic interview skills with children and young people can be found in Copley and Forryan (1987).

CONCLUSION

It is hoped that in this chapter the case has been established for teachers attempting to engage in dialogue with pupils who display behavioural and emotional difficulties with the aim of helping those pupils gain greater insight into the nature of their difficulties and their behaviour. In the course of this it is hoped that something has been done also to demystify dynamic psychotherapy. It has not been the intention to suggest that teachers should take on the role of psychotherapists or rush out to engage in in-depth exploration of all their pupils' emotional lives. Indeed, an understanding of dynamic psychotherapy should foster caution in entering into such relationships with troubled children.

Rather it has been done with the aim of establishing that the principles of dynamic psychotherapy can be readily translated into meaningful and realistic terms for all teachers. The approach may appear initially to have more relevance for those working in special schools where the whole environment can be geared to foster its aims, but it has equal value for teachers working in less 'special' settings. For if dynamic psychotherapy is, as Brown and Pedder suggest, all about 'a conversation which involves listening and talking with those in trouble' (1979, p. x) then this is something which all teachers can, and indeed do, do in all schools, even if the extent to which this happens varies. No matter what its value is in more specialised work, at the very least, dynamic psychotherapy provides teachers with a means of making that conversation more effective.

4

BEHAVIOURAL APPROACHES

It is not perhaps surprising that behavioural psychology has had a considerable influence on approaches to work with children and adults with emotional and behavioural difficulties. Although much of its early experimental base concerned work with animals rather than people, learning theory has, as Walker (1984) puts it, 'spawned a collection of practical measures known as behaviour modification, or behaviour therapy, which have made a significant contribution to such areas as the treatment of severe neurotic phobias and the education of handicapped children' (p. 2). Indeed, applications of the behavioural approach have not been confined to such areas of severe and complex problems but have also been reflected in teaching in ordinary schools. The term 'behaviour therapy' is usually applied in a more limited way to the clinical techniques of desensitisation and modelling.

Systematic desensitisation involves gradual exposure to a hierarchy of stimuli which have previously provoked great anxiety. The patient is trained to relax and the technique is based on the theory of 'reciprocal inhibition', that this ability to relax will inhibit the previous fear response. If there is any agitation at all the exposure is promptly terminated and only started again once relaxation has been re-established and earlier stages in the fear hierarchy worked through again. Herbert (1978) describes practical application of desensitisation in treatment to counteract school phobia, with successively greater involvements with school, supported by the attendance and support of a parent or therapist.

Modelling, or observational learning, seeks to teach a new

73

pattern of behaviour by getting the patient to observe another person demonstrating the desired behaviour with successful consequences. This technique has been used to improve social skills in coping with bullying, dealing with interviews and resisting pressure to engage in anti-social activities (Herbert, 1978). Sometimes observation is followed by role play to practise the new repertoire of behaviours in a non-threatening situation.

BEHAVIOUR MODIFICATION

Behaviour modification has been defined as 'a process in which some observable behaviour is changed by the systematic application of techniques that are based on learning theory and experimental research' (O'Leary and O'Leary, 1972, p. 17). Characteristically a programme of behaviour modification will begin with a precise definition of the behaviour to be changed so that it can be quantified and counted as a 'target' to be increased or decreased. Incentives will then be judiciously used to encourage and reward desired behaviour, whilst undesired behaviours are ignored so that they will 'extinguish' for want of reinforcement or, if necessary, the frequency and intensity of undesired behaviour is punished by aversive consequences.

Learning theory distinguishes between two classes of behaviour: respondent and operant. Respondent behaviour consists of reflexive and involuntary reactions such as sweating, salivating, shivering. In Pavlov's classic experiment, the response of salivation was conditioned in dogs to become not only a natural response to food but eventually a conditioned reflex to an associated stimulus in the form of a buzzer. Through this and other experiments, Pavlov (1927) reached the conclusion that training, education and discipline of any sort were nothing but a long chain of conditioned reflexes. But as Walker (1984) persuasively argues, Pavlov did not take sufficient account of the specially human characteristic of language and its influence in shaping behaviour of the other class, voluntary or operant behaviour such as talking, walking, eating. These behaviours are most influenced not by a stimulus before they occur but by the consequences which follow their occurrence. Behaviour which results in a pleasant consequence will be reinforced and therefore is likely to be repeated whilst behaviour which is followed by an unpleasant consequence is likely to diminish.

Applied to dealing with pupils with emotional and behavioural difficulties, behaviour modification means that problems should always be described in terms of behaviour rather than personal attributes or attitudes. As the child's behaviour is not conceptualised as being caused by internal drives and forces but rather shaped by the effect of external cues and reinforcers, the behavioural approach looks outside the child to the classroom environment and learning experiences to find ways of changing behaviour. This places responsibility firmly with the teacher for specifying behaviour which should be changed, counting and charting its frequency; setting goals for improvement; breaking these goals into smaller steps which can be taught and reinforced; checking whether these goals are attained and evaluating whether the programme of modification is successful, if necessary changing cues and reinforcers until success is achieved. In short, any problems with behaviour are the teacher's responsibility not the child's fault.

Specifying behaviour

This responsibility begins with defining behaviour in a clear and specific way. Often descriptions of behaviour are so vague or so influenced by personal interpretation that problems in communication inevitably occur between teachers themselves, as well as between teachers and pupils. Bull and Solity (1987) quote the example of the different reactions of two teachers to a pupil who smiles on being reprimanded: to one teacher this is an 'insolent' response, to the other a sign of 'nervous' embarrassment. They argue that 'the behavioural approach and its concern with the observable can help us to make sure that our own reactions to events and our communication of these to others are as accurate as possible' (p. 6).

All too easily, vague descriptions of behavioural characteristics can become diagnostic labels and 'worse still, such labels are sometimes used as if they are explanatory constructs' (Herbert, 1978). Much time can be wasted on what Ross (1968) has called the 'Rumpelstiltskin Fixation'. Psychologists and teachers become preoccupied with semantics, believing that if

75

they give the correct name to a condition, their problem will be solved, instead of getting on with the task of teaching. Thus, much time and effort may be spent on deciding whether a child is 'hyperactive' or 'dyslexic' or 'disruptive' rather than working out how best to help the child to sit still, read more fluently or stop calling out when the teacher is talking.

Even if they do not lead to an unproductive, tautological confusion between symptoms and labels, imprecise or 'fuzzy' descriptions of a behaviour make it difficult to count and chart its incidence. It is therefore essential to define the 'target' behaviour in terms of action or performance, which can be seen, and agreed to be seen, by separate observers. Thus 'aggressive' or 'hostile' behaviour is better described in terms of the number of times the subject hits out or swears at other pupils.

Measuring behaviour

Having determined what is the exact behaviour to be studied, the next step in a programme of behaviour modification is deciding on a system for recording the frequency, duration or intensity of the 'target' behaviour. Given the availability of a colleague to act as an observer, a structured schedule such as OPTIC (Observing Pupils and Teachers in Classrooms) developed by Merrett and Wheldall (1986) might be used, but measurement, particularly a straightforward frequency count of how often a behaviour occurs, can easily be made by an individual teacher. Scherer (1990) discusses a variety of means of frequency recording, from simply jotting down on paper to more elaborate digital counters for marking every time a behaviour occurs. For recording the duration of a behaviour or for 'interval sampling', seeing whether a behaviour is happening at particular set times during a period of observation, a stopwatch and probably some sound alarm to prompt the observer will be necessary. The intensity or seriousness of a behaviour is more difficult still to record, needing either video recording or some judgement by the observer on a rating scale from 1 (hardly noticeable) to 10 (unbearable). As Scherer suggests this judgement is likely to 'drift' if teachers get used to, or become more tolerant of, the behaviour which is being recorded.

Whichever system is adopted, recording will provide a

'baseline' against which the success of any intervention can be measured. Sometimes the very action of recording, particularly if pupils are aware of what is being observed and whether it is viewed favourably or not, may prompt changes in behaviour without the need for further intervention. On other occasions the act of recording may give the teacher a different sense of proportion about misbehaviour. Actually counting the number of times the problem occurs can provide the reassurance that a behaviour is not so frequent or intense as it had appeared to be. Often seemingly irrational responses can be explained by the circumstances which prompt them, once these are discerned by careful observation.

If, however, the teacher does decide to proceed with a programme of modification, then the baseline will provide a measure of that programme's success. Usually this evaluation will take the form of a design in which a baseline is taken by recording the number of times a behaviour occurs in several lessons. This might, for example, chart the number of times a pupil calls out, or runs around the classroom, or the percentage of time interval observations when a pupil is 'on task' or 'off task' (with these behaviours much more specifically defined for the purpose of the investigation). After this baseline has been established an intervention is then tried and the same behaviours measured to see whether their frequency, or rate of occurrence, has been altered. If proof is sought that it is the intervention rather than some other variable which has produced the effect then returning to the baseline condition can check whether it is in fact the intervention which is making the difference. For example, if a child's habit of getting out of his or her seat and interfering with other children's work appears to have been reduced because of being praised and rewarded for remaining in place and on task, then terminating the praise and rewards would be expected to result in a return to the earlier unsettled behaviour. Whilst obviously important in establishing the experimental evidence to underpin behaviourist theory, in practice the intention is to maintain any new behaviour rather than reverse it. In the classroom, measurement will usually be used to check that more desired behaviour is increasing and that it is continuing to be rewarded.

Setting goals

The successful use of behaviour modification is well documented (Herbert, 1978 and Bull and Solity, 1987, give references to many sources) but it is an elaborate process and one which requires a considerable investment of teacher time. It is important, therefore, that the technique is applied towards attaining worthwhile goals. Emphasis on observable behaviour should not mean emphasis on trivial behaviour and concern with reducing unwanted behaviour should not mean a concern with negative rather than positive aspects of behaviour.

In establishing goals it is important to consider the long-term development of social skills and not merely the encouragement of short-term conformity. Two ways in which this can be done are through linking any behavioural intervention to a broader programme of personal and social development and ensuring that goals are positively framed for teachers as well as pupils.

Scherer (1990) argues that traditional responses to disruptive behaviour have been limited by their 'crisis intervention' approach, which focuses on getting rid of an immediate problem. He suggests that a better approach would be a preventive model, which identifies the social and study skills required for successful learning. Devising a list of classroom behavioural and social skills should provide an opportunity for teachers to examine expectations and develop consistency across the school.

Scherer (1990) offers a Schools Skills Checklist as a basis for assessment and this could be used as a starting point for discussion. This lists specific behaviours which demonstrate appropriate skills in areas such as starting, getting on with and ending lessons, presenting work, interacting with pupils and teachers, responding to praise, criticism, teasing and bullying. The checklist is completed by the teacher noting whether in each of these areas the skill is displayed 'as a normal pupil', less than or more than a normal pupil or if a particular behaviour is 'not applicable' or 'not known'.

With regard to setting behavioural goals, these skills are then broken down into smaller observable sub-skills, for example some of the elements of getting on with the lesson are: stays in appropriate place; puts hand up and asks quietly for teacher to assist; completes set work; requests next task. Thus, Scherer's checklist provides both a form of assessment of assets and deficits in social skills, offering the basis for teaching behaviours which will avoid problems arising and also, even if starting with 'crisis intervention', a way of placing short-term goals within a wider context of personal and social development.

Burland (1990) describes how a special school for boys with emotional and behavioural difficulties developed a social skills training strategy using behavioural techniques to provide pupils with a package of 'survival skills' for life within a comprehensive school. Though designed for youngsters embarking on a programme of reintegration, the package is a very useful source of good advice for any pupils on strategies for improving social interaction in areas such as greeting, being polite, giving and accepting praise, avoiding teasing and bullying and being popular with peers. As with Scherer's checklist, the particular value of Burland's strategy is that it offers a context in which goals for behaviour modification can be part of a broad developmental and positive perspective.

An essential part of setting positive goals is the importance of defining and promoting desired behaviours which are incompatible with undesired behaviours rather than merely endeavouring to reduce the latter. Using behaviour modification to shape teacher performance as well as pupil response is another aspect of goal setting. Wheldall and Merrett (1992) use the term 'positive teaching' to describe their behavioural approach, which advocates increasing teacher praise and approval and decreasing teacher disapproval and reprimands. They quote studies which they have made showing that teachers used praise more than disapproval in response to academic behaviour but, whilst quick to remark on social behaviour of which they disapproved, teachers hardly ever voiced approval of desirable social behaviour so that it appeared that children were expected to behave well without the need for praise but were continually reprimanded if they did not! Wheldall and Merrett divide their recommendations for encouraging positive teaching into the use of antecedents (or cues) and consequences (or reinforcers).

Arranging cues

A cue is a signal which prompts or guides a course of action. Bull and Solity (1987) analyse three components of the classroom environment which contain cues which predispose pupils to behave in particular ways. The physical component is the classroom surroundings and its assortment of furniture materials and equipment. The social component is the teaching style and grouping arrangements. The educational component is the curriculum content and selection and presentation of learning tasks. There is much in common here with studies of classroom management from a more eclectic perspective (see Chapter 6) and it is interesting to note also that Wheldall and Glynn (1988) have coined the term 'behavioural interactionist perspective' (BIP) to describe their integrating the use of naturally occurring learning experiences, through which teachers and pupils learn from each other, as a new perspective on the application of methods and principles of behaviour analysis in the classroom.

Examples of behavioural analysis of classroom antecedents, or 'setting events' as Bull and Solity prefer to call them, are studies of the physical component as in seating arrangements, where 'on task' behaviour increased for children sitting in rows rather than around tables (Wheldall, Morris, Vaughan and Ng, 1981) or was influenced by whether boys and girls sat together or separately (Wheldall and Olds, 1987); of the social component where, in classes for young children, combining teacher touch with praise increased work involvement (Wheldall, Bevan and Shortall, 1986) and of the educational component where the amount of time junior school children spent reading was increased when quiet reading was modelled by their teacher (Wheldall and Entwistle, 1988).

The statement of clear rules and expectations, combined with the establishment of a series or tariff of consequences for non-compliance associated with 'assertive teaching' (Canter and Canter, 1976), is another aspect of arranging cues to shape appropriate behaviour from pupils and again this topic is explored further in Chapter 6. The more effectively children learn to respond to environmental cues and understand how to discriminate, which behaviours are required in different settings, the more easily they will generalise these skills to other similar, but different, tasks, but this learning will take place more quickly if appropriate behaviour is suitably rewarded.

Providing reinforcement

Positive reinforcement occurs when events that follow a behaviour strengthen its frequency, duration and intensity. Skilful teachers give effective rewards and arrange pleasant consequences without resort to what Wheldall and Merrett (1992) dub 'behavioural overkill' in the use of heavy, intrusive reinforcers which are difficult to maintain. Neisworth and Smith (1973) provide a helpful concept in terms of a reinforcement hierarchy with, at its base, the management by others of tangible reinforcers but above that, reinforcement through social approval of others, at a higher level self-managed reinforcement, through permitting oneself relaxation or more pleasurable activity after a job is completed, and at the highest level, self-generated reinforcement, such as the well-being which comes with the satisfaction of a job well done. In schools, teachers aim for the higher levels of reinforcement, but start with approval and praise and resort only if necessary to tangible reinforcement. As Rogers (1991) puts it 'the ultimate goal of all external reinforcement is the natural reinforcement enjoyed as a result of appropriate behaviours'(p. 197).

To be effective in shaping behaviour, social approval, or tangible reward, must be contingent upon clearly identified behaviour and will be most powerful if it follows the target behaviour as soon as possible. This is easy enough with praise, 'Thank you for putting up your hand, I like the way you're working quietly, well done.' It is not so easy to immediately deliver a tangible reinforcement, but using tokens, such as stars or points, to be exchanged later for a reward or reinforcing event, can provide an acceptable symbolic alternative. Deciding on what are suitable rewards through negotiation with a class can be an enlightening experience and, if delivery of tokens is always paired with praise, that association can rapidly become as important as the tangible reward and ease the path upward through the reinforcement hierarchy, towards social approval being sufficient in itself.

Token reinforcement, or token economy as it is usually described, enables teachers to use a behavioural approach with groups, individuals within which might be working towards a variety of different goals and motivated by a variety of different rewards. For some children a more formal behavioural contract may be a more powerful procedure. Gurney (1990) describes such a contract as both a process, involving negotiation, and a product, in the form of a written agreement. Teacher and pupil discuss and formulate an agreement on changes in the behaviour of both parties. Usually this involves the teacher arranging a specific reward such as extra time on a favoured activity which is made contingent upon the pupil's improved work performance, greater punctuality or some other reasonable and attainable target. This agreement is then written out and signed by all parties. Gurney quotes successful examples of contracting and discusses essential features which contracts should include, such as details of desired behaviour change, rewards, penalties and duration, with clear procedures for data collection, resolving disputes and re-negotiation. These examples suggest that contracts are most effective when kept fairly short, with modest and readily attainable goals. He emphasises the point that teachers should not enter discussions with preconceived ideas or assumptions about the pupil's motivation or seek to impose a contract which they think is suitable. Gurney argues that contracting must be a reciprocal process and it gains its greatest strength from the improved commitment of a pupil, whose viewpoint is taken seriously and who therefore experiences a sense of partnership within the enterprise.

Evaluating success

However they are delivered, whether directly or by token, reinforcers will show an effect within a relatively short period of time. No intervention can be expected to solve all behaviour problems at once. However, if clearly defined target behaviours have not increased within a treatment phase equivalent to the baseline period then the programme must be reviewed. Evidently the rewards have been insufficiently powerful or the rearrangement of antecedent events has failed to cue the desired response. Steps can be taken to review rewards or revise classroom arrangements but it may also be necessary to consider punishment if misbehaviour is proving intractable.

Punishment in behavioural terms occurs when aversive, unpleasant events follow a behaviour with the intention of reducing its frequency. In school, punishment may take many forms: criticism, reprimands and telling off, yelling, shouting, imposition of extra work, detention or inflicting physical pain, though smacking and corporal punishment are not officially condoned. In an extreme situation, where a child's behaviour is personally dangerous or so disruptive that it interferes with the progress of a lesson, punishment may be necessary to suppress or deter the misbehaviour in the short term. However, though effective in stopping a bad behaviour, punishment alone will never start a good one and there are other side effects which require consideration.

Children observing that teachers get their way by being hurtful to others, may 'model' this behaviour, retaliating in kind directly or showing similarly aggressive behaviour towards their weaker classmates. Emotionally, punishment is likely to evoke dislike and anxiety causing children to become unco-operative and unwilling to contribute to lessons, preferring the safety of a passive role to the excitement of more active learning. Children may learn ways to avoid punishment through deceit or cheating, or escape a threatening situation by not turning up for lessons. For all these reasons punishment does not find favour in behavioural theory save as a last resort which may buy time and opportunity for a more positive approach. Certainly if evaluation shows that the use of punishment is increasing then, whatever the initial intention, it is not being effective. This may be because, however aversive the punishment was thought to be, in practice 'unofficial reinforcement' from increased attention and enhanced status with other pupils may outweigh the apparent unpleasantness which has been inflicted. To respond to this by increasing the harshness of the punishment may have emotional costs for the teacher in terms of disquiet and stress heightened by an antagonistic classroom atmosphere.

This issue of personal cost must be an element in any evaluation of a programme of behaviour modification. The object of the exercise is to make teaching and learning more pleasant and enjoyable. If the teacher is enjoying the experience then the pupil probably will be as well, but the converse is equally likely to be true. Evaluation should show that the investment of time and energy in behavioural engineering is producing a good return in academic achievement and social competence, but there should also be significant if less tangible improvement in the classroom climate. In other words, the implementation of a behavioural approach should have evident rewards and positive reinforcement for the instigator as well as the recipients of the programme. If this is not happening, if the teacher feels that too much time is spent checking the recording clipboard with too little time for communication, or that setting the stopwatch leaves too little time to smile, or that the distribution of tokens is becoming a source of dispute rather than delight, then either there is a breakdown between behavioural principles and practice or behavioural theory has not been correctly applied.

5

SEEING PROBLEMS IN CONTEXT

The subject of this chapter is the ecosystemic approach to emotional and behavioural problems in schools. This is a relatively new approach, originating from the work of American scholars and practitioners (e.g. de Shazer, 1982; Molnar and Lindquist, 1989), and developed in the form described here by two of the present authors (Upton and Cooper, 1990; Cooper and Upton, 1990a, 1990b, 1991a, 1991b, 1992). In fact the approach is new enough to provoke Josh Schwieso (1992, p. 91) to ask:

> [. . .] what would lead teachers to prefer what is, as the authors [Cooper and Upton, 1992] admit, a relatively untried enterprise [i.e. the ecosystemic approach] to one that has amply proved its worth [i.e. the behavioural approach]?

There is a simple answer to this question. New ways of thinking about behaviour problems may lead to new ways of dealing with behaviour problems. At the very least this will add to range of possibilities available to the teacher who is faced with a problem situation. Furthermore, this approach combines aspects of disparate traditions in its recognition of the value of behavioural analysis, along with a stress on the importance of interpersonal relationships more often associated with humanistic psychology. This places the ecosystemic approach within the humanistic tradition of British education, which emphasises the need for schools to be run on democratic, person-centred lines, with their ultimate goal being the development of autonomous, self-directing individuals. It argues that teachers, and consequently schools, in order to be 'effective', must give prominence to humanistic principles in their daily practice (Cooper, 1989). The approach can also be seen in the context of the current concern for increased school effectiveness, as exemplified in the recent Elton Report on discipline in schools (DES, 1989a), and in the increasingly important role of teachers as guardians of children's rights, as a consequence of the 1989 Children Act (Bridge and Luke, 1989). Tyler (1992) suggests that such a distinctively humanistic educational psychology offers an alternative to those who find certain aspects of behaviourism depersonalised and dehumanising. It is the humanistic dimension which distinguishes the present approach from the behaviouristic 'ecological perspective' proposed by writers such as Swap, Prieto and Harth (1982).

In this chapter, the authors describe an ecosystemic approach, and its development. Examples of application are then given, in an attempt to identify the potential value of the approach to teachers and schools. It is suggested that:

1   the ecosystemic approach offers new ways of thinking about behaviour problems in schools, which are based on the view that human behaviour is developed and maintained through interactional processes;
2   the ecosystemic approach, described by the present authors, offers teachers a new range of strategies for dealing with emotional and behavioural problems, which emphasise collaborative approaches to problem solving, and the central importance of individuals' particular ways of thinking about problems in the development of solutions;
3   the ecosystemic approach offers specific and practical measures which may lead to the enhancement of the overall effectiveness of schools, stressing as they do the power that is derived from the appreciation of differing, sometimes conflicting, personal perspectives on situations, and the importance of giving consideration to human individuality. This approach not only offers assistance to students and their teachers, but also has important implications for relationships among staff and between staff and parents.

There is, as yet, only limited research evidence to support the effectiveness of the ecosystemic approach in schools. Molnar and Lindquist (1989) describe a range of intervention strategies, and give examples of their use by American school personnel (teachers, counsellors and psychologists) who have received brief in-service training in the techniques. The foundation of the ecosystemic approach, however, lies in the field of family therapy, the literature on which abounds with case study examples of the successful use of intervention strategies based on interactional principles, with families where presenting conditions include: eating disorders, sexual dysfunction, violent behaviour, bed-wetting and obsessional behaviour. There is also evidence of successful work by psychologists and therapists with problem behaviour in schools, where they have acted as consultants to the school system (e.g. Power and Bartholomew, 1985; Taylor and Dowling, 1986).

Before describing the approach, it is necessary to say something about its origins. The approach draws on family therapy sources, but is informed by a specifically educational perspective, which emphasises the distinctive qualities of the school/classroom situation, and the existing specialised skills of teachers. It should be stressed that the approach does not propose any kind of simplistic analogy between the classroom and the family. It is also important to emphasise that it is not suggested that practising teachers can or should develop the level of skill and expertise possessed by trained family therapists. The approach simply proposes that it might be possible for teachers to make profitable use of systemic insights, and particular intervention techniques which follow from these insights, in their everyday interactions with students, students' parents/families and colleagues.

THE ORIGINS OF THE ECOSYSTEMIC APPROACH

Systemic theory and recursive causality

The ecosystemic approach to human behaviour is founded on the notion that the origins and purposes of human behaviour are essentially interactional. The main idea is that human beings are social beings, who are as dependent on the social environment for their mental well-being, as they are on the physical environment for their physical survival. According to this view, human beings are neither wholly free, in an existential sense, to behave as they choose, nor is their behaviour wholly determined by environmental forces. Human beings exist within a social web, rather like a biological ecosystem, in which the individual's behaviour and development is both constrained by, and a constraining force upon, the behaviour and development of others with whom s/he interacts. From an ecosystemic viewpoint, human behaviour is the product of ongoing interaction between influences in the social environment and internal motivations which derive from prior (mainly social) experience. Furthermore, the overarching, twin human needs for a recognised personal identity and a sense of social belonging make the social group (or 'system') the central focus of human activity, to the extent that individuals' personal needs and motivations are often subordinate to those of the group as a whole. The potential for conflict, both interpersonal and intra-personal, in such circumstances is obvious. All group members depend upon the group to supply particular needs, thus the maintenance of the group is paramount, even if its maintenance requires the sacrifice of one of its members.

The theoretical origins of this view of human behaviour rests in the work of Ludwig von Bertalanffy (1950, 1968) and Gregory Bateson (1972, 1979), and in the clinical practice of pioneer family therapists, such as Selvini-Palazzoli *et al.* (1973), Minuchin (1974) and de Shazer (1982, 1985). Von Bertalanffy is responsible for the original formulation of 'General System Theory' (von Bertalanffy, 1950, 1968). A central tenet of this theory, of particular relevance to classroom problems, concerns the interconnectedness of elements within a system, and the connections between systems. When applied to social systems (e.g. the family), it emphasises the ways in which changes in any one part of the system (e.g. the relationship between parents) will reverberate throughout the system (i.e. have consequences for the children of the family), and may lead to reverberations in allied systems (e.g. the school). Family therapy techniques are based on the social application of this and other systemic principles.

Family therapy

Bateson was among the first to apply a systemic approach to the realm of mental health and family functioning. Bateson *et al.* (1956) published a highly influential paper which reported the presence of recurrent patterns of communication in the families of diagnosed schizophrenics, which, they argued, served to promote and maintain the symptomatic behaviour. A central concept introduced in this paper is that of the 'double bind', which describes the way in which diagnosed schizophrenics were observed to be required by their families to fulfil contradictory demands, the fulfilment of any one of which represents the breaching of another (e.g. behaving with hostility towards the symptomatic individual, then behaving in a loving manner when the individual responds negatively to the initial hostility). In short, the symptomatic individual is placed in a 'no win situation', in which the outwardly irrational behaviour characteristic of schizophrenia can be interpreted as a rational response to the double bind. The motivation for placing and maintaining the symptomatic individual in this situation is that it provides the family as a whole with a stable communication pattern which masks other family pathologies (e.g. a decaying marital relationship) which threaten the survival of the family system. The schizophrenic individual is constructed by the family group (with his or her unwitting compliance) as a problem which deflects attention from other difficulties and also provides a focus of activity which the family can share without engaging in conflict which may threaten the family's survival. Thus the double bind can be viewed in terms of a strategy which promotes what the family perceives as manageable conflict, in place of what is perceived as unmanageable conflict: manageable conflict is encouraged, whilst unmanageable conflict is avoided.

The logical consequence of this formulation is that symptomatic behaviour (e.g. schizophrenia) becomes an integral part of family functioning, and particularly of interactional patterns in the family. It therefore follows that the unit of treatment, in such situations, should be the family of the symptomatic individual, rather than that individual alone (as in traditional psychiatric practice). It is this contention which forms the basis of the practice of family therapy.

The perspective offered by the present writers draws on three major approaches to family therapy (Speed, 1984b), each of which emphasises particular elements in the ecosystem of family dysfunction (that is, a particular range of influences on inter-actional events). These approaches are not mutually exclusive, and are often combined by therapists. The aim of therapy is always to promote positive change in the family system which enables the family to function effectively and without the need for the destructive interactional patterns that have grown up around the symptomatic individual. Each therapeutic model offers a systemic analysis of interpersonal interaction in families, and together they provide us with a range of analytical tools for developing systemic analyses of classrooms and other inter-actional systems.

The first of these approaches to family therapy is that provided by the Milan group (Selvini, 1988), which advocates that therapists should focus on those conflicts which the family system is attempting to avoid. Therapists, therefore, devote considerable energy to the development of systemic hypotheses which account for the symptomatic behaviour in terms of family functioning. The purpose of therapy is to bring these conflicts to the surface and devise behavioural strategies which the family can perform in order to resolve them.

The second approach is referred to as the Structural approach (Minuchin, 1974). Here the emphasis is on family structure. It is argued that a major source of family dysfunction is to be found in inversions and distortions in the family hierarchy (e.g. where the child in a nuclear family takes on a parental role and becomes the key decision maker). These distortions lead to contradictions between actual and expected behaviour, with family members overtly claiming to act in accordance with a family structure (e.g. claiming that the parents are the key decision makers) which their actions covertly distort. An important structural concept is that of 'boundary', which describes the degree of separation between members of a system (e.g. family). Where boundaries are too rigid, members become 'disengaged' from one another, and communication between members is diminished; where boundaries are too weak, 'enmeshment' develops, and members become incapable of achieving the necessary distancing they require for the development of their individual roles and identities. Structural therapy aims to restore the family system to a more appropriate structure which asserts the appropriate hierarchical and boundary relationships.

The third approach is referred to as Strategic therapy. Strategic therapy places particular emphasis on the interactional sequences which surround and maintain the symptomatic behaviour (Watzlawick *et al.*, 1974; Madanes, 1981) and, more recently, on areas of family functioning in which problems are dealt with successfully, with a view to adapting successful problem-solving behaviour to less tractable problems (de Shazer, 1982, 1985; Molnar and de Shazer, 1987). The key tenet of this approach is that change in any part of an ecosystem produces change throughout the system. Strategic therapists focus on specific situations in which problem behaviour occurs (or does not occur), and their aim is to devise strategies which family members can use which give negative feedback to problem behaviour and encourage the development of new and sustainable patterns of interaction. Some strategic therapists (e.g. Madanes, 1981) argue that by giving families strategies which lead them to make behavioural changes, family members are led into a process which forces them to confront underlying, masked conflicts. Essentially, however, strategic therapists are less overtly concerned with uncovering these masked conflicts (unlike therapists), preferring to focus on specific situations in which problem behaviour is manifest.

The challenge faced by all systemic family therapists is to help families to establish new interactional patterns which 'fit' the family system, and so appear to the family members to be appropriate to their needs. Family therapists do not attempt to impose solutions upon their client families; they instead seek to activate patterns of interaction which are already available, though hitherto unexplored or simply dormant, in the existing family system. This is a particularly difficult task, because the systemic nature of interactional patterns means that they have a self-perpetuating, circular (i.e. 'recursive') quality, in which cause and effect cannot be objectively isolated. Individuals caught in such patterns, which they feel to be destructive, often feel powerless to effect change, believing their own behaviour to be rational and inevitable. Strategic therapists often locate problem-maintaining behaviour in that very behaviour which family members have devised as problem-solving behaviour. The therapist is, therefore, often attempting to lead family members to a point where they will dispense with a pattern of behaviour which has developed in relation to particular circumstances pertaining to the family. This gives rise to the essential character of systemic therapy, which is that it promotes change through the use of non-lineal (and often 'indirect') intervention strategies. These non-lineal strategies do not overtly challenge problem behaviour, but rather seek to change the behaviour by rendering it ineffective in the eyes of family members, with the result that they dispense with the behaviour of their own choice. This often involves readjusting family members' perceptions of their behaviour through the prescription of tasks which lead clients to a new perspective on their behaviour. Such readjustment, however, can only be successfully achieved when the therapist is able to frame the new perspective in terms of the family members' personal systems of meaning; that is, family members have to be shown why, according to their own values and perceptions, such a readjustment is called for.

There is much overlap between the three main approaches, and practising therapists often combine elements from different approaches (Hoffman, 1981). It has been suggested that some of the apparent theoretical disagreements between the groups can be attributed to the different client groups with which each school of therapy chooses to work (Speed, 1984b). The Milan group, for instance, worked most often with the families of individuals with life-threatening or severely psychotic conditions (e.g. schizophrenics, anorexics), whilst strategic therapists tend to work with more common disorders, such as bed-wetting, marital disharmony and sexual dysfunction, which, though apparently mundane by comparison, are often equally intractable. For our purposes there are a number of principles under which the various approaches to family therapy unite:

1 the aim of therapy is to promote positive change in situations characterized by interactional patterns (i.e. patterns of feedback and reinforcement, by which particular behaviours are perpetuated or suppressed) which are harmful to one or more of the family members;

2 this makes the interactional system (i.e. the family or part of the family) the focus for intervention, rather than any

individual member, since it is the system which functions to maintain the undesired situation;

3 successful change depends upon the quality of 'fit' between the chosen intervention and the existing pattern of family functioning (i.e. the intervention must be an alternative pattern of behaviour which is perceived by the family or family subsystem as viable);

4 accurate knowledge of the pattern of family functioning is only achieved by a therapist who is willing and able to form a co-operative relationship with family members, and is, in effect, able to 'join' with the family to create a therapeutic system which facilitates the exposure of the interactional patterns surrounding problem behaviour, and the perceptions and personal meanings underlying them;

5 the need for the therapist to control personal bias and to achieve both a detached and deepened understanding of the family situation is facilitated by the use of a therapeutic team, whose presence is often hidden behind a two-way mirror during therapy sessions, and results in the generation of additional and often divergent perceptions of what they observe. This 'poly-ocular view' (de Shazer, 1985) promotes creativity which is necessary for the generation of appropriate interventions;

6 once an appropriate intervention is put into action, the feedback mechanisms in the family system take over, and thus a new interactional pattern is established. The therapist is no longer required, having facilitated a positive solution which utilises the family's inherent capacity for self-regulation.

AN ECOSYSTEMIC APPROACH TO SCHOOL BEHAVIOUR PROBLEMS

A significant proportion of the work of family therapists is concerned with childhood behaviour problems. It is not surprising, therefore, that in recent years many family therapists (particularly in America) have begun to focus some of their attention on the school system as a factor in family difficulties which manifest themselves in childhood behaviour problems. Lindquist *et al.* (1987) suggest that school-related problems are best characterised in one of three ways, as (a) a problem in the family that disturbs the school, (b) a problem at school that disturbs the family or (c) a problem at school that does not disturb the family.

Smith (1978), Worden (1981) and Okun (1984) all describe ways in which students' problem behaviour in school can sometimes be related to difficulties in the family system, particularly in terms of 'triangulation'. Triangulation describes a relational triad in which two members form an alliance against the third. This can take the form of an over-close relationship (what structural therapists call 'enmeshment') between a student and parent, at a time when there is marital disharmony. The student is oversensitised to the anxieties of one parent, and the object of the other's hostility. The student's symptomatic behaviour (e.g. disruptive behaviour at school) serves as a diversion for the family in times of parental disharmony, and creates the circumstances which enable the parents to behave as an apparently 'normal' family (i.e. with parents co-operating in reaction to stress apparently created by their child's misbehaviour at school), with the student's misbehaviour in school serving as a rationalisation for the over-closeness in the parent–child relationship. In these circumstances the major source of family disharmony (the parental dyad) is left unacknowledged, and attention is focused on the student's behaviour. Another important family–school triangle is the parent–child–teacher triangle (Guerin and Katz, 1984; Okun, 1984), in which a parent–child conflict is displaced to the teacher–student relationship. In these circumstances school-based intervention is unlikely to achieve a lasting solution, and family therapy is called for. Worden (1981) suggests that a child's behaviour problems in school can often be seen as an indication of a clash of values or roles between the two systems. Hsia (1984) describes how families' often 'paralysed' response to the highly disturbing symptoms of school phobia can be indicative of underlying family difficulties which serve to sustain and promote the child's phobic reaction. In all of these cases, family interactional patterns are serving to maintain the students' symptomatic behaviour. The focus of intervention in these circumstances, therefore, becomes the family of the symptomatic pupil, rather than the pupil alone.

In Britain, Dowling and Osborne (1985) have developed what they describe as a 'joint-systems' approach to a wider consideration of the school ecosystem, seeing the school as an important influence on the pupils' behaviour. They therefore advocate that family therapists act as consultants to the school system as well as the family system, as appropriate. Taylor and Dowling (1986) and Dowling and Taylor (1989) describe the setting up of an outreach service, whereby a group of family therapists make themselves available, on a regular basis, to parents and teachers by basing themselves on school premises. Campion (1985) also advocates the training of British educational psychologists in family therapy techniques, as a means of bringing families and schools into closer harmony. Provis (1992), more recently, describes the use of systemic approaches for dealing with school behavioural problems, in the context of a British LEA schools psychology service.

In America, Molnar and Lindquist (1989) have described a school-focused approach, which involves classroom teachers and other school personnel using systemic techniques in the normal course of their work. Molnar and Lindquist's work is particularly apposite at the present time in Britain, coming as it does in the wake of the Elton Report (DES, 1989a), since it takes as its focus the need to provide teachers with techniques for dealing with oppositional pupil behaviour of the type identified as being most prevalent in the national survey commissioned by the Elton Committee (Gray and Sime, 1989). These behaviours are termed 'oppositional' because they represent deliberate and repeated infringements of classroom rules which teachers impose in order to create what they believe to be the necessary conditions for effective teaching and learning to take place.

The main problem with the types of behavioural difficulties described here is their persistence and apparent resistance to the approaches which teachers most commonly use to oppose them (e.g. reasoning, punishment, ignoring, detention, discussion, withdrawal, referral to another teacher, withdrawal of privileges (see DES, 1989a, p. 240)). These (essentially 'lineal') approaches, far from changing the problem behaviour, can serve to maintain and promote the behaviour they seek to alter. The ecosystemic approach of Molnar and Lindquist, however, seeks to offer teachers the means to change the problem behaviour, not by challenging the behaviour overtly, but by utilising the systemic principles which sustain interactional patterns. One of the major aims of their approach is to assist teachers in redefining oppositional behaviour in terms which lead both teacher and perpetrator to see the behaviour as co-operative or positive, rather than oppositional or negative. Deprived of a barrier against which to kick, and presented with a new and undesired rationale for the negative behaviour, the behaviour loses its original effect and is therefore made redundant (this point is exemplified in the section headed 'Intervention').

The very act of developing a new perception of the negative behaviour can itself remove the teacher's desire to change the behaviour though, more often, it is the projection of this new perception which leads the pupil towards a conscious decision to change the behaviour pattern. Thus the pupil's determination to behave according to his/her own value system, and not to be merely obedient to the teacher's wishes, is employed by the teacher as a means of controlling the pupil's behaviour. For this reason the approach has been referred to as employing '"judo" principles' (Mandel et al., 1975). The key point is, however, that behaviour problems are resolved without loss of face and without the pupil surrendering behavioural autonomy. This makes the approach particularly appropriate to classrooms in which qualities of autonomy and self-direction are valued pupil traits, which may be threatened by approaches to problem behaviour which demand the pupil's open surrender of auto-nomy in subservience to the teacher's authority.

As yet, there are no published examples of the use of such interventions in British schools. There is, however, a growing number of reports and articles describing the successful use of such strategies in American schools. Mandel et al. (1975) describe the successful use of such techniques with EBD pupils in a special school who swear, and are belligerent towards teachers. Others describe the successful use of such techniques in main-stream schools, with pupils who present physical aggression towards other pupils (Brown, 1986), tantrum behaviour (Amatea, 1988), fighting, in-school truancy, depression with suicidal tendencies (Williams and Weeks, 1984), school phobia/school refusal (Hsia, 1984). Molnar and Lindquist (1989) also describe the use of these techniques with a wide range of behaviour problems commonly encountered in mainstream schools, such as: lack of attentiveness, chronic 'gossiping', apparent inability to settle down to work, failure to complete homework and classwork assignments, talking out of turn, interrupting the teacher, belligerence towards teachers and pupils. They also describe instances in which teachers employed the techniques successfully with problematic colleagues.

KEY COMPONENTS OF THE ECOSYSTEMIC APPROACH TO SCHOOL BEHAVIOURAL PROBLEMS

Below is an exposition of some of the key features of the ecosystemic approach to school behaviour problems (see also Upton and Cooper, 1990):

1 Problem behaviour in the classroom does not originate from within the individual who displays the behaviour, but is a product of social interaction.

2 Interactional patterns may be conceptualised in simple or complex ways. The simple analysis is confined to here-and-now situations, and will define a student's negative behaviour in terms of the interactions which immediately surround this behaviour. A complex analysis will take into account factors in the wider ecosystem, and explore purposes which the here-and-now behaviour might serve in other, related ecosystems. Such an analysis may relate oppositional behaviour in the classroom to interactional patterns in the student's family.

3 The cause of any instance of problem behaviour is part of a cyclical chain of actions and reactions between participants. Each event in the interactional chain is both a cause of ensuing events and the effect of preceding events. Student classroom behaviour which is defined as 'problematic' is always goal directed, and from the student's viewpoint it is understandable, rational and, above all, necessary. What appears problematic to the teacher may well be the solution to a problem for the student, for a subsystem in the classroom or school, or the student's family. Attempts to directly oppose goal-directed behaviour inevitably meet with resistance, and can, therefore, help to encourage the problematic situation to continue. The repeated use of failed solutions, in this way,

is often characteristic of apparently intractable systemic problems.

4 Intervention, based on an ecosystemic analysis, must recognise the contribution made to the interactional events surrounding a problem, by *all* participating parties. This emphasises the reflexive quality of the ecosystemic approach, which requires teachers to analyse their own behaviour, and its relation to the perceived problem. Teachers can only influence their students by eschewing confrontational approaches and entering into a co-operative relationship with them, in which the 'problematic' behaviour is reconstructed in terms which are meaningful to both the student and the teacher (and members of significant subsystems, such as family members, other students, school personnel, where appropriate), and which reveal one or more of the following things:

a the goals served by the behaviour;
b the inappropriateness, for the student, of the goals that are or may be served by the behaviour;
c alternative/more effective means of achieving the goals which the behaviour is perceived to serve.

In constructing a picture of a problem situation, it is necessary for the teacher to establish awareness of his/her phenomenological interpretation of the situation, and to set this against those of others involved, particularly students. The teacher must identify in specific behavioural terms: (a) the precise nature of the problem as s/he sees it, in terms of repeating behavioural patterns, the times, places and individuals involved, (b) possible positive interpretations of the problem behaviour and (c) how the situation will be different when improvement begins and after the problem is solved. This involves the teacher in a degree of self-analysis, in which evidence for the existence of the problem is amassed and scrutinised, along with the teacher's behavioural expectations. Molnar and Lindquist (1989) describe this process as 'sleuthing'. A vital component of the process involves the teacher in seeking perspectives on the situation other than his/her own, particularly those of the students involved. Molnar and Lindquist suggest that teachers be alert to students' use of figurative language in their descriptions of problematic situations. Since it is through figurative language that we make personal sense of the reality around us, it follows that teachers will communicate more effectively with students if they make use of their figurative language, and use this as an exploratory tool in defining situations from the students' viewpoint. Teachers must also be constantly alert to positive changes, however apparently insignificant, which occur in the classroom ecosystem, whether or not they appear to be related to the problem situation or not. Such minor changes may give rise to hitherto unthought of solutions.

INTERVENTION

The chief characteristic of recurring problem situations is their apparent self-perpetuating inevitability. Individuals believe themselves to be behaving in the only rational way that is possible in the given circumstances. For instance, a teacher reprimands a pupil who disobeys her, the pupil responds to the reprimand with abuse; the teacher reprimands the pupil further; the pupil abuses the teacher further, and so on. Each is driven by the conviction that not to confront the other's reprimand/abuse, is to accept the unacceptable. A distinguishing characteristic of ecosystemic intervention is the use of 'divergent explanations of problem behaviour' (Molnar and Lindquist, 1989, p. xv). Such divergent explanations seek to redefine problem situations so that conflict (or resistance) is seen as co-operation. This tenet holds true in any social ecosystem, whether it be (for example) the interactional dyad of the pupil and teacher, the mesosystem (i.e. the interaction among systems) of family and school, super-power and super-power.

As has already been noted, behaviour which functions to maintain an individual's symptomatic condition can often be seen, from a systemic viewpoint, to be serving a goal else-where in the system. Power and Bartholomew (1985) present a case study involving a student with learning and behaviour difficulties, in which parent–school enmity is seen to be a predominant factor. After a period of sustained conflict between the school and the family, a family therapist was brought in as consultant. The therapist developed the following interpretation of the situation. The student was seen by his teachers to be underachieving, and his parents appeared to be using their son's difficulties as a diversion from their marital problems. The parents were able to unite with one another in their concern for their son's problems, and this helped to prevent marital break-up. Consequently, the parents had a vested interest in maintaining their son's difficulties, and did so by opposing the school's efforts to solve their son's problems, through, for instance, over-protectiveness and encouraging him not to complete homework assignments. Teachers at the school responded to what they saw as family collusion by being unsympathetic towards the student, and making unrealistic demands upon him. The school–family relationship was seen to be characterised by a pattern of symmetrical interaction, 'that is, one in which each party responds to what the other is doing in a similar way' (p. 223). Such relationships are founded on constant competition for the dominant position. Thus, in the present case, the teachers' suggestion that the student's school problems were related to the family circumstances, would be met by the counterclaim that the teachers were not working effectively. It is the nature of such relationships to escalate, leading to deeper entrenchment on both sides, with each party undermining the efforts made by the other to help the student. The chief loser here, ironically, is the student.

Clearly, such a conflictual situation would be unlikely to produce a solution to the student's difficulties. The consultant family therapist proposed an intervention which sought to convert this symmetrical relationship into a complementary relationship. A complementary relationship is characterised by non-competitive interaction, so that, for instance, dominance is met with passivity, anger with appeasement, etc. The consultant persuaded the school personnel to be compliant with the parents' views at the next meeting, and to adopt a subordinate role. When, during the meeting, the parents became hostile towards the school staff, the social worker took up the parental position, and presented it in an exaggerated form, suggesting that their son should be relieved of all pressures in class. The parents responded to this in a conciliatory manner, and for the first time they suggested that 'the teacher did have the right to place some expectations on the students in her class' (p. 226). This was a point at which the parents and staff were in agreement for the first time. The deadlock was broken, and an opportunity to develop a collaborative relationship was established. The eventual outcome of this case was that the parents and the school personnel agreed to recognise the primacy of each other in their respective domains. The teachers agreed not to pressurise the student in class, and, instead of setting specific homework tasks in addition to classwork, they agreed to allow him to take uncompleted classwork tasks home. It was agreed that whether he completed the tasks at home was a matter for the parents to decide, and the school would simply award the appropriate grade without placing any pressure on the student. By allowing the student to take classwork home, the school was enabling the parents to control the 'pressure' their son was placed under. This newly collaborative relationship between the school and the family also led to their accepting advice from a psychologist on aiding their son with stress management. Thus the student's therapeutic needs were met, as were the parents' needs for a collaborative activity with one another (i.e. as a diversion from their marital difficulties), and the school's position was also validated.

A key feature shared by ecosystemic intervention strategies, and demonstrated in the above example, is that, when they succeed, individuals change their behaviour and become more co-operative with others, whilst retaining their sense of control over their own behaviour. For example, the parents in the above example, when faced with an overly compliant response, found that it was necessary, for their own purposes, to support the school position, and soften their dominant stance. They stated that they wanted the school to place a certain amount of pressure on their son, even though this had been a major source of disagreement earlier. This point emphasises the ecosystemic idea that it is the patterns of interaction among people which maintain problematic situations, rather than the situation which appears to be the focus of the problem. The purpose of ecosystemic intervention techniques is to offer participants the means to break out of destructive cycles of interaction, through the creation of new cycles. This is demonstrated repeatedly by Molnar and Lindquist (1989), in their exemplification of eco-systemic techniques for classroom teachers and other school personnel.

The archetypal ecosystemic technique, described by Molnar

and Lindquist, is that of 'reframing'. The technique is based on four basic propositions: (i) we behave in accordance with the way in which we interpret problem situations, (ii) there are often many different but equally valid interpretations of any given situation, (iii) change our interpretation and we can change our behaviour and (iv) change in our behaviour will influence the perceptions and behaviour of others.

For example, a teacher may seek to reprimand a student, in order to prevent him/her from repeatedly talking out of turn; the student, however, might persist with the deviant behaviour regardless of the increasing severity of the reprimands. Without knowing that pupil's perception of the situation, the teacher is still able to effect change in the ecosystem by changing her own perceptions and behaviour. The teacher's behaviour is clearly based on the interpretation that talking out of turn is a deviant act. The reframing technique requires the teacher to seek a new, plausible and positive interpretation of the behaviour, through the process of 'sleuthing' (see above), and then to behave in strict accordance with this. For it is essential that the reframing be feasible and believable in the eyes of the pupil. Such an interpretation might be that the student often interrupts the teacher in order to seek clarification for particular points made by the teacher. The behaviour is now defined as a positive service to the class as a whole.

For the intervention to be effective, the teacher must behave in strict accordance with the reframing. In order to do this the 'symptom prescription' technique (Molnar and Lindquist, 1989) might be used. This involves the teacher encouraging the student to perform the symptomatic behaviour in revised circumstances. The teacher might suggest to the student that s/he increase the frequency of interruption in order to optimise the value of the service it provides.

The successful outcome of such intervention would be that a situation of conflict has now become one of co-operation. As with the antagonistic parents, referred to above, the apparent concession by a former adversary may give rise to complementary concessions. On the other hand, it could be said that control of the problematic behaviour has now passed from the student to the teacher. Where the behaviour may have been perceived in the past as means by which the student gained control over the teacher (by 'winding him/her up') it has now become a means by which the teacher exerts control over the student. In any event, talking out of turn is now redundant as a tool for engaging in conflict; to do so now is in fact perceived as an act of co-operation. The likelihood is that the student will cease the behaviour, and possibly take up another form of behaviour which achieves the initial goal of the interrupting behaviour.

Molnar and Lindquist provide many examples in which interventions of this sort succeed, and they repeatedly suggest, on the basis of anecdotal reports of teachers using such approaches, that the seed of co-operation that is planted in such situations often has a transforming effect on the quality of interpersonal relationships involved: students with whom teachers have experienced difficulty in forming co-operative relationships, become more amenable and generally much easier to get along with. Such observations require careful consideration and experimental scrutiny. As they stand, however, these observations suggest a number of interesting hypotheses as to the effect of ecosystemic approaches on the social climate of the classroom, which would seem to be in line with research which has shown the considerable influence of teacher expectations on pupil performance and behaviour (e.g. Hargreaves *et al.*, 1975).

In order to demonstrate this approach, an observational study, conducted by one of the present authors in an English special school, will be presented. This study will be used (i) to demonstrate an ecosystemic analysis of classroom behaviour and (ii) to indicate intervention strategies that might arise from such an analysis. It should be stressed that this is a theoretical demonstration. Whilst the classroom events described were actually observed, the interventions were not applied, and were not communicated to the teacher involved. It should also be stated that the authors recognise the classroom events described here to be of an extreme nature. This lesson contained by far the worst examples of classroom disharmony observed throughout a four-week period in which the researcher visited three schools. These events are not typical of the daily life of schools in Britain, and must not be considered as such. This extract is presented because we believe it to illustrate, graphically, certain key issues in the ecosystemic approach, which appear, in a less heightened form, in classrooms throughout the education system.

A CASE STUDY

The following interactional sequence was observed in a special school for pupils of secondary age with emotional and behavioural difficulties. The school operated a behavioural programme, by which pupils could obtain privileges in accordance with their performance on a range of criteria, which was constructed in consultation with pupils and formalised in terms of a 'contract'. Teachers passed on the pupils' contracts to one another when lessons changed, and at the end of each lesson teachers awarded each pupil a mark (out of 10) for his/her performance in accordance with the contract terms. The lesson involved a group of four 3rd-year boys, who were being taught by an experienced special needs teacher who had been at the school for approximately six months. The teacher had given the pupils a worksheet to complete; all four pupils had been working fairly calmly for several minutes when the following sequence took place. Throughout the sequence the teacher maintains the outward appearance of calmness and composure, and employs a calm and patient voice. (Names and other analytically irrelevant details have been altered.)

(Note: 'P' refers to 'Pupil'; P1 is also referred to as 'Carl'; 'T' refers to 'Teacher'.)

P1: [puts pen down emphatically] I'm not doing this, it's boring.
P4: Yeah, it's boring.
T: [calmly] If you are not on task you are going to lose points. You may get a nought.
[P4, pushing worksheet away, turns to P3 and they begin a conversation.]
P1: [pushing worksheet on floor, fiercely] I don't care. I'm not doing this boring, shit work. [Gets out of seat and makes for the classroom door, which he opens.]
T: If you go out of the room, you will get a nought on your contract.
[T gives P1 a stern look, to which he responds with an impish grin, as he stands provocatively, holding the handle of the open

door; looking as if he might step out of the room at any time.]

T: Sit down Carl, and do your work.

[P1's grin fades to an aggressive scowl, as he moves away from the doorway and begins to roam the classroom with apparent aimlessness.]

T: Sit down Carl, or I'll have to give you a nought.

P1: Balls!

T: If you're off task, I have to give you a nought; you know that.

P1: Fuck off!

T: Carl, I want you to get on with your work.

P1: Fuck off, you bitch.

[P2 looks up from his work occasionally to see what is going on, but continues to work for the most part. P3 is by turns working and scuffling with P4, who has not resumed working. P3 and 4 stand up as if to fight.]

T: [to P3 and 4] Okay you two, you're off task; that's going to be nought, unless you get back to it.

[P3 and P4 exchange conspiratorial grins. They make as if to square up to one another. They sit down. P4 kicks a chair, sending it loudly spinning across the room. Meanwhile P1 has returned to the door; has opened it, and is hanging out of the doorway into the corridor.]

P1: I'm fucking off.

T: I've told you, if you go out of the classroom, you're going to get nought on your contract.

P1: So. If I want to go, I go. You can't stop me.

T: [to P1] If you don't do the work now, you'll have to do it later, at home. [NB: this is an established practice within the school.]

P1: Fuck off.

[P1 starts to roam the room again. P4 picks up his worksheet, screws it up and throws it. The missile hits P1, who retrieves it and throws it. The teacher is in the line of fire, and is hit.]

P1: [looking genuinely surprised and apologetic] Sorry Miss! [T gives P1 a stern look. P2, 3 and 4 snigger silently, behind the T's back] I didn't mean it to hit you. [P2, 3 and 4 are now seated; apparently working.]

T: Right, that's a nought for you Carl. [Writes on a piece of paper.]

P1: That's not fair!

T: What do you expect?

P1: Fucking cow! Bitch!

[*P1* sits down and angrily starts to write on a sheet of paper, which he then violently destroys.]

P1: I'm not doing it. It's rubbish. [Scatters torn fragments over the floor.]

T: You're just going to have to do it later.

P1: Fuck off! [*P1* stands up and kicks his chair hard against the wall. He starts to walk around the room again. *T* deals with a query from *P3* about the worksheet. *P1* goes over to *P4*; they start to tussle; this time a little more seriously than before. *T* interposes herself between them.]

T: [firmly] Stop that!

P4: [sits down] Give us another worksheet then.

[*P1* is still standing in front of the teacher, in a confrontational stance. There is a sense of mockery in the stance, but only just. *T* walks away from *P1*. *P1* follows, muttering barely audible swear words, the most audible of which is 'fuck'. *T* does not react. *P1* bumps into teacher.]

P3: Ooh! Carl's going to rape Miss!

[*P2* and *4* laugh.]

P1: [to *P3*] Fuck off, you cunt! Fuck off!

[There is a loud noise in the corridor. *P1* goes to the door and opens it.]

T: [sharply] Don't go out there! I told you . . .

P1: Fuck off! I'm not staying here! [He leaves the room and does not return.]

This interactional sequence illustrates the principle of circular causality in that the teacher and Carl repeatedly challenge one another in an attempt to assert their individual definitions of the situation. At whichever point we choose to punctuate this interactional sequence we can identify both Carl's behaviour as a cause of the teacher's behaviour, and the teacher's behaviour as the cause of Carl's behaviour. Both are attempting to assert their will over the other and to avoid giving in to the will of the other. The teacher's choice of control strategies appears to be based on the assumption that she is in a position of authority over Carl. From the start, it is clear that Carl does not accept this definition of the situation. Carl's determination to assert his refusal to recognise the teacher's authority stimulates the teacher to continued attempts to assert her authority (through the use of commands and threats), which in turn stimulate Carl to further displays of resistance, and so on, in a relentless circle of assertion and counter-assertion. This circle of causation rapidly develops into an escalating spiral ('symmetrical escalation', see above), which is exemplified by Carl's increased use of verbally offensive language (swearing and insults) and provocative posturing ('roaming' behaviour, standing in the doorway, confrontational stance), with a corresponding escalation in the teacher's assertion of authority (at first threatening sanctions calmly, then firmly and finally applying one of the threatened sanctions).

Both the key actors in this sequence attempt to influence one another's behaviour in a lineal manner, that is, they appear to perceive one another's behaviour in terms of 'either/or logic' (de Shazer, 1985). They see only the alternatives of accepting or rejecting the behaviour of the other. An ecosystemic approach recognises that, in a self-perpetuating situation such as this, neither alternative is appropriate, since both alternatives produce conflict which is unacceptable to one or other of the parties involved. What is required, in such a situation, is for one of the parties to behave differently, but in a way which still appears to be rational to both parties.

In the present example an appropriate systemic technique might be that of 'reframing'. The art of reframing is to produce an alternative meaning for a particular behaviour which is equally convincing to all those involved in the interaction. In the present example, opportunities for reframing are offered to the teacher by those aspects of Carl's behaviour which he clearly perceives to be oppositional. For instance, when Carl first leaves his seat and goes to the door as if to leave, the teacher immediately responds with a threat of punishment. The teacher is, therefore, implying that she frames Carl's behaviour as oppositional. A suitable reframing might involve defining Carl's behaviour not as a sign of assertiveness, but rather as an expression of vulnerability and, as such, a stimulus for sympathy rather than punishment. The teacher might suggest to Carl that whilst such behaviour is normally forbidden, that Carl's special vulnerability and sensitivity to the classroom situation make his desire to leave understandable, and his inability to control this urge worthy of sympathy. The teacher may even go on to suggest that Carl's behaviour serves a positive function for the teacher ('positive connotation of function', Molnar and Lindquist, 1989), in that it reminds the teacher of the need to take particular care when dealing with a pupil as specially sensitive as Carl clearly is. The teacher may also suggest that the behaviour reveals a positive motive ('positive connotation of motive', Molnar and Lindquist, 1989), in that it leaves the teacher free to devote more time to the remaining pupils, and so reveals a tendency towards a self-sacrificing nature: a trait which exemplifies Carl's sensitivity to others' needs. Another approach might be for the teacher to suggest that Carl leave the room at other times during the lesson for a period specified by the teacher ('symptom prescription', Molnar and Lindquist, 1989).

In selecting an appropriate intervention, it is essential that the teacher take into account the pupil's likely response to the chosen intervention. On the basis of the present example, for instance, it would seem that Carl is unlikely to wish to behave in ways that make him appear 'vulnerable' or 'sensitive' (i.e. this would run counter to the aggressive 'macho' image he projects), whilst the unsettled and excitable behaviour he exhibits make such an explanation feasible. Furthermore, once the teacher has made such a case, and behaves in accordance with the reframing, the pupil is faced with the alternatives of continuing his current pattern of behaviour, and so supporting the reframing, or ceasing the behaviour pattern and so confounding the teacher's reframing. Either way, the teacher has gained ascendancy. If the pupil continues to misbehave he is merely proving the teacher right, and allowing her to express empathy and understanding; if the pupil ceases to misbehave, then the teacher's strategy has led to a restoration of order. Given the tendency of such oppositional pupils as Carl towards assertiveness (Mandel *et al.*, 1975) it is more likely that he would seek to take the latter course.

From an ecosystemic viewpoint, the intervention strategies outlined above would gain particular force from the fact that they would represent a change in the interactional pattern. The present extract, coincidentally, offers an example of the power of such an unexpected change. When the worksheet-missile inadvertently strikes the teacher, Carl is suddenly apologetic, and refers to the teacher, for the first time, as 'Miss'.

The intervention hypothesised above might be termed a 'simple' ecosystemic intervention (Upton and Cooper, 1990), in its avoidance of any enquiry into the motivations of the participants. Though, of course, a teacher working autonomously would intervene only after having subjected her personal construction of the situation to critical scrutiny, and with consideration of what is known of the student's viewpoint. A more complex intervention, which might be necessary if classroom-based intervention proved ineffective, would entail a more detailed enquiry, possibly by a family therapist. In conversation with the teacher involved, after this lesson, the researcher remarked with admiration on the teacher's self-control and display of patience. The teacher responded to this by saying that she was able to behave in this way because she firmly believed that such a conflict situation did not represent a problem for her, but was rather a problem internal to the student. She believed that all she could do in such circumstances was to remain patient and firm, but that it was outside her capability to change such situations. She remarked, philosophically, that at other times she seemed to get on quite well with Carl; this had been one of those occasions when Carl was in one of his moods. A question that might be fruitful to ask here would be if a different way of thinking by the teacher might produce a different pattern of teacher behaviour, and thus lead to changes in pupil behaviour. It might be possible, for instance, that the teacher's declared emotional neutrality is experienced by the pupil as a form of provocation. Whether the pupil sees it this way or not might be less important than the effect of this suggestion on the teacher's own thinking.

Unfortunately, Carl was unavailable for interview, as staff felt that he required a cooling off period. It is important to note, however, that Carl's condition, for several hours after this event, is best described as distraught. It was suggested by members of staff, however, that Carl's reaction might be related to what was generally perceived to be his lack of respect for women. It was noted that he was in the care of his single mother who, staff felt, was easily manipulated and bullied by her only son. Whilst the teacher's negative framing of the situation would support the feasibility of the intervention proposed above, the information relating to Carl's background might indicate that the problem be tentatively characterised as 'a problem in the family that disturbs the school' (Lindquist *et al.*, 1987), and thus appropriate for a joint systems approach (see above).

CONCLUSION: TOWARDS A NEW EDUCATIONAL PERSPECTIVE

An ecosystemic approach seeks to define behaviour problems in schools in terms of the interactional systems which maintain and promote behaviour. This approach rejects ways of conceptualising behaviour problems which see the problem in terms of a quality or defect of the individual. As such, the ecosystemic approach is in keeping with the wealth of research evidence which describes the ways in which schools and teachers unwittingly engage in the construction of 'deviant' pupils (Keddie, 1971; Hargreaves *et al.*, 1975; Sharp and Green, 1975; Reid, 1985). These and other writers argue that it is the quality of interpersonal interaction between teachers and pupils, in many of our schools, that produces students who are disaffected and actively resist their teachers in return for what they see as the degradation and ill-treatment that characterises the daily routines in many schools (Hargreaves, 1967; Rosser and Harré, 1976; Woods, 1976; Tattum, 1982; Schostak, 1983; Cooper, 1993). These writers draw on the testimony of pupils to make the case that disruptive behaviour in schools can often be seen as a rational response to intolerable circumstances (see also Chapter 7, this volume).

The ecosystemic approach offers a mechanism for analysing and changing interactional patterns, that can be employed by individuals at the dyadic level, as well as at larger institutional levels. The vital importance of the school–family interactive system, which has long been seen as an important area for development in British education, particularly in relation to learning and behavioural difficulties (DES, 1978; Reynolds and Sullivan, 1979; Galloway, 1985a; Galloway and Goodwin, 1987; DES, 1989a), is also recognised by this approach, and practical measures for overcoming some of the difficulties encountered in this area are suggested.

In these important areas the ecosystemic approach can be seen to indicate new avenues for research and application. It is envisaged that such work would provide a valuable addition to that which is already being done by some advocates of other approaches (e.g. Wheldall *et al.*, 1983; Wheldall and Merrett, 1984; Wheldall, 1987; Wheldall and Glynn, 1989), who are concerned to promote the development of learning environments which are more responsive to the needs of school students, through the sensitisation of teachers and parents to the influence they can have on the behaviour of students.

In looking to the future of the ecosystemic approach, and its application to British education, we see certain important contextual factors of which account must be taken. The first is what we see as the humanistic tradition in British education, which can be traced back to the early writings of A. S. Neill (Neill, 1916), through the child-centred movement of the 1960s (DES, 1967), the development of student-initiated learning approaches (Barnes, 1976), and into the contemporary concern for democratic schooling (Fletcher *et al.*, 1985; Harber and Meighan, 1989). In a recent micro-sociological study, Cronk (1987) has shown how a humanistic approach to classroom behaviour problems can lead to an improvement in students' classroom behaviour and lesson involvement. Central to Cronk's approach is the importance attached to the sharing of phenomenological constructs of the classroom situation between pupils and teachers. This clearly relates to Molnar and Lindquist's (1989) concept of 'sleuthing'. We suggest that the effectiveness of such 'sleuthing', the aim of which is to gain an understanding of students' phenomenological worlds, would be enhanced if the 'sleuths' were trained in some of the counselling skills of humanistic psychology, which involve the development of empathy through the exercise of skills, such as active listening, reflection and paraphrase (Rogers, 1980; Mearns and Thorne, 1988). The absence of empathic understanding between teachers and students would seem, from a reading of the literature on school behaviour problems referred to above, to be a major factor in the development and maintenance of behaviour problems. The use of empathy by teachers would add to the reflexive quality of the ecosystemic approach with regard to teacher behaviour, by encouraging teachers to continually analyse the experience of schooling from the student's standpoint.

A second contextual matter relates to the role of the

mainstream classroom teacher in British schools. Concern has been expressed in recent years about the way in which support staff, delegated to mainstream schools to act as consultants to mainstream teachers in the support of pupils with special educational needs, have been increasingly used by mainstream schools in the role of peripatetic specialist teachers. Galloway and Goodwin (1987) have suggested that this situation has had the reverse effect to that of its original intention, and has resulted in the 'de-skilling' of mainstream teachers in the SEN area. This can be seen in the broader context of increased specialisation in the teaching force, in which teachers' roles become evermore precisely defined in terms of specialist skills and responsibilities. Galloway (1985a) has suggested that the pastoral effectiveness of some schools has been undermined by the development of separate pastoral systems, which have the twin effects of identifying certain teachers as having specialist pastoral responsibilities, whilst excluding other 'non-specialist' teachers from the performance of pastoral functions. In the face of such tendencies towards 'de-skilling' we suggest that the ecosystemic approach offers skills which mainstream teachers could develop through INSET, as Molnar and Lindquist (1989) have described.

Whilst the examples of ecosystemic interventions described by Molnar and Lindquist would appear to be well within the capabilities of appropriately trained mainstream teachers, those joint systems interventions, which involve school and family, would clearly remain within the province of the specialist family therapist. We would suggest, however, that the training of teachers in ecosystemic approaches will make teachers more aware of the potential value of family therapy and, therefore, more likely to seek the support of family therapists, in the context of the type of outreach model described by Taylor and Dowling (1986) and Dowling and Taylor (1989).

Molnar and Lindquist (1989) provide a range of techniques which they claim can be easily assimilated by teachers, who can use them autonomously and to great effect. One of the key features of the ecosystemic approach is a recognition of the power that can be derived from different perspectives on a situation. With this in mind, it would seem that the ecosystemic approach might develop in the context of staff support groups (as recommended by the Elton Committee), with access to a specialist family therapist (and/or educational psychologist trained in family therapy), who could perform the dual roles of professional supervisor and training consultant. Peer group support would facilitate the development of new perspectives on difficult situations, and have valuable social implications for teachers, who often feel professionally isolated in these matters. The availability of a specialist consultant would also help teachers decide when it was appropriate to hand cases over to specialist therapists. In these ways the ecosystemic approach offers teachers a range of possible solutions which begin to recognise the vast complexity which lies behind some of the more intractable behavioural problems they face in the classroom. The approach offers teachers a new range of skills as well as suggestions for the necessary in-school and out-of-school support, that are designed to improve the quality of the all important three-way communication and interaction between teachers, pupils and parents.

6

CLASSROOM
MANAGEMENT

Practising any profession involves a combination of 'craft' experience and 'technical' theory. As far as classroom management is concerned, there has often been a tendency to ascribe success to personal charisma and 'on the job' learning at the chalkface. Whilst these are undoubtedly contributory factors, research and observation have also identified techniques in lesson organisation and teaching style which can be articulated as a theory of classroom management. However, in doing this there are hazards in avoiding the Scylla of abstraction and the Charybdis of the commonplace. On the one hand, teachers may complain that psychological and sociological terminology elevates discussion to an inappropriately rarefied level divorced from the everyday reality of the classroom. On the other hand, research may be dismissed for merely restating tricks of the trade, normally acquired through personal experience.

Mongon and Hart (1989) suggest a categorisation of books on behavioural difficulties in schools which reflects this divide. The majority of books on this topic, they claim, belong to one of two categories: the 'general critique', providing analysis of definitions, statistical information and insight into general issues and the 'teacher handbook' offering specific guidelines and tips for teachers. Perhaps this categorisation oversimplifies a little, with most authors in this genre attempting some integration of theory and practice, research and application but their call for a framework from within which problems can be tackled is a valid one. The question is, how to structure that framework. Elements of such a conceptual framework are offered by Frude (1984), Smith and Laslett (1993) and Wolfgang and Glickman (1986).

CONCEPTUAL FRAMEWORK

The first element, taken from Frude (1984), proposes a framework for considering research on disruptive behaviour based on three levels of analysis: incidents, individuals and interaction. At the *incident* level research focuses on the classroom looking at what happens when a disruptive incident or event occurs. Why do such events occur, what triggers them and why do they escalate? How do pupils and teachers ascribe different meanings to incidents? As was suggested in Chapter 1 a number of authors have pointed out that much behaviour characterised as disruptive or maladjusted by teachers may be seen by its perpetrator as a normal and rational reaction to provocation. Research such as that carried out for the Teacher Education Project (Wragg, 1984) demonstrates the value of close observation of transactions within classrooms which can show how effective teaching skills can avoid precipitating such incidents.

At the *individual* level, disruption can be related to personal characteristics of pupils and teachers. This involves examining differences in personality types, teaching and learning styles and attitudes to learning. What are the characteristics which make some teachers 'deviance-provocative' and others 'deviance-insulative' what are the qualities which [...] (Wood, 1984)?

[...] attached to the [...] are intended

[...] to how schools [...] certain types of [...] How do some [...] control whilst [...] on co-operation [...] er such limited [...] hat some pupils [...] by resorting to disruption and [...]

The second element of a framework [...] ysis of techniques in classroom management is offered by Smith and Laslett (1993) where effective management is related to four complementary aspects of teaching: management, mediation, modification and monitoring. Though not sequential and in practice often over-lapping, there are different skills required in each of these areas, which can also be related to Frude's concept of intervention at different levels. Management refers to skills in lesson organisation and presentation. It is focused on what Frude would describe as the incident level, analysing different elements and phases of classroom activity. Mediation and modification can be seen as focusing on Frude's individual level, referring to ways in which teachers provide counselling, guidance and, where necessary, programmes for shaping and changing behaviour through the use of suitable rewards and punishments. Monitoring is the term used to describe the process by which schools check the effectiveness of policies on discipline and pastoral care and see whether interactions are positive.

The third element drawn from Wolfgang and Glickman (1986) shows how individual decisions about aspects of teaching can be related to a continuum of teacher behaviour and to teachers' beliefs about discipline. The teacher behaviour continuum which they describe extends from non-interventionist approaches to very firmly interventionist action. At one end of the continuum, teachers use only supportive and accepting responses intended only to help pupils work through their problems for themselves. At the other end of the continuum, rewards and punishments are used to correct misbehaviour. How far teachers move along this continuum will depend on their beliefs on discipline.

Wolfgang and Glickman describe three schools of thought about discipline in schools, similar to the perspectives outlined in earlier chapters, associated with psychoanalytic (see Chapter 3), social (compare Chapter 4) and behavioural psychology (see Chapter 5).

The 'Relationship–Listening' school takes the view that the child develops from an inner unfolding of potential and that the job of education should be to provide a facilitating environment, which enables the expression of feelings. If there are difficulties in school then the teacher should have faith in the pupil's ability to wrestle with, and solve, problems. The teacher would counsel by listening, reflecting back feelings, avoiding judgement or direction but trying to help pupils take control of their own destiny. This perspective draws on the Freudian psychoanalytic model which sees inner drives as destructive, but also on the Rogerian humanistic model which takes a more positive view of any pupil's inner rationality, arguing that education 'builds upon and around the student's natural desire to learn' (Rogers, 1969).

The 'Confronting–Contracting' school takes the view that the child develops from the interaction of internal and external forces. Education should make pupils aware of behaviours that enhance or detract from social acceptability. If difficulties arise then the teacher should clarify responsibility for finding a mutually acceptable solution. From this viewpoint, teaching is not simply about releasing pupil potential but about a series of interactions between teacher and pupil in which conflicts cannot be resolved without shared responsibility (Dreikurs, 1968). This perspective draws on the cognitive developmentalist psychology of Bruner (1966) which argues that growth is a matter of external pull from society as well as internal push from the individual. The teacher counsels by confronting children with the consequences of their actions and working out a plan or contract for improvement.

The 'Rules/Rewards–Punishment' school takes the view that the child's development is conditioned by external forces. This view draws on the behaviourist promise that adjustment in behaviour is determined by the environment. Education should provide a controlled environment which shapes the social and academic skills required by society. If difficulties arise then it is the teachers responsibility to find a solution by changing rewards or punishments so that the pupil's behaviour is modified. Indeed 'teachers who do not bring about suitable changes in student behaviour are failing to live up to the responsibility of the profession'. This perspective draws on the premise of behaviourist psychology that external reinforcement and rewarding consequences shape and change behaviour (Skinner, 1971).

Bringing together the three perspectives of levels of analysis (Frude, 1984), aspects of teaching technique (Smith and Laslett, 1993) and personal beliefs on discipline (Wolfgang and Glickman, 1986) offers a conceptual framework for examining the practical application of theory in classroom management.

INCIDENT MANAGEMENT

Difficulties in classroom management derive from incidents which can escalate from minor irritation to major confrontation if not handled appropriately. In order to reduce or avoid disruptive incidents it is useful to apply what have been described by Smith and Laslett as the 'four rules' of classroom management: get them in; get them out; get on with it; and get on with them. Effective teachers 'get them in' by starting lessons smoothly and promptly, not only getting pupils into their places on time but also tuning them into the lesson itself. Providing short, simple tasks which recap the previous lesson or give a reminder of the skills needed for the next activity offers a reassurance that new learning will be within the pupil's competence. Whilst the class is engaged in this work the teacher has time to deal with registration or other administrative duties and to cope more easily with the petty irritations of lost or malfunctioning equipment. Too slow a start to a session can lead to a reluctance to begin work at all; too demanding an opening to a lesson can lead to a feeling that, as the topic is well beyond the learner, it is hardly worth trying at all.

The ending of the lesson is another time when disruptive incidents are likely to arise, so it is important to match activities to levels of ability. Teachers who 'get them out' efficiently, give thought to the orderly routine with which they conclude their work, tidily and unfussily collect materials and dismiss their pupils but also make sure that every opportunity is taken to refresh, restate and reinforce the theme of the lesson.

The pupil's sense of competence and self-esteem in a particular subject area depends to a great extent on how successfully teachers manage to 'get on with it', in the sense that they maintain the momentum of lessons by selecting suitable content and ensuring that it is delivered with appropriate variety and pace. Many problems in management are avoided if there is detailed scrutiny of the suitability of textbooks and learning activities for mixed-ability teaching. Too often work is set for a notional mid-ability range which leaves the most able unstretched and the least able untouched. Providing alternative and supplementary materials will help avoid disruptive incidents.

Where there are specific difficulties in reading and writing, help can be given through providing topic summaries and study guides which identify and explain key words and concepts. Alternative methods of response, such as tabulating information, labelling and subdividing texts, offers a change from traditional essay or comprehension exercises. Working in pairs or small groups can be a valuable experience of co-operative learning as well as providing support for pupils whose ability might otherwise be underestimated because of literacy problems. These methods should reduce the possibility of disruptive incidents arising from pupils' feelings of frustration or inadequacy.

Working with groups, rather than only dealing with the class as a whole, helps with the fourth rule of classroom management: 'get on with them'. This refers to techniques which help teachers build good personal relationships with children through becoming more aware of them as individuals. Some pupils can easily fade into anonymity as part of a class of thirty but are immediately more visible when they are being dealt with as part of a group of five or six. This makes it easier to learn names and gather information about individual characteristics, making it easier to ensure that every pupil is able to achieve that sense of progress and competence so essential to encouraging continued effort even in the face of difficulties.

Working with groups involves considerable planning of physical arrangements as more flexible arrangements inevitably increase the potential for disruptive incidents. Classroom layout or design may need rethinking to set up 'learning centres' or 'resource islands' so that groups can work in turn on particular aspects of a topic, and to facilitate movement around the room. The growth of mixed-ability teaching, often involving an element of group work, has increased the potential for disruptive incidents from sources of friction such as 'talking out of turn' or 'hindering other children'; these were the categories of disruptive behaviour most frequently encountered by teachers, reported in a series of studies of disruptive behaviour (Wheldall and Merrett, 1992). Calling out when not called upon, chattering about non-work-related matters and making unwanted comments or remarks are all much easier when groups working at tables are partly masked from supervision. More fluid group

activities present greater opportunities for unauthorised movement and interference with the work of other pupils. Coping
with incidents such as these, teachers employ a range of preventive rules and routines and responsive techniques which
deflect, or defuse, the effect of disruptive behaviour.

Rules define the boundaries for permissible behaviour and
reduce the likelihood of friction, provided that they are fair and
not 'obscure, arbitrary or petty rules which discredit the whole
code' (DES, 1989a). Ideally rules should reflect an agreed consensus on what is essential to ensure polite communication,
personal safety and proper respect for the rights of others.
Routines regulate the flow of activities within the classroom and
provide a predictable pattern and sequence for learning experiences. They should mark out the phases or stages of a lesson, so
that a demonstration or talk is followed by practice, with settled
arrangements for distributing and collecting materials, moving
around the room and seeking help and advice when needed.

INDIVIDUAL MEDIATION AND MODIFICATION

Applying the four rules of classroom management and developing effective rules and routines should reduce the sources
of friction within a classroom. Where individuals do misbehave,
a teacher's response will reflect personal beliefs on discipline
but, whatever these may be, the nature of the response is likely
to move along a continuum according to the perceived seriousness of the interruption.

Wolfgang and Glickman (1986) suggest a continuum in which
interventions progress from a child-centred to a teacher-centred
model of responsibility, power and control: 'At one end of the
continuum, strategies are used whereby the child has most
control of his or her behaviour and the teacher has minimal
control . . . at the other end of the continuum the teacher sub-
sumes the child's power' (p. 22).

Redl and Wineman's (1952) description of techniques for the
manipulation of surface behaviour outlines a similar progression
of response to misbehaviours which are more likely to derive
from attention seeking or warding off inadequacy than any more
deep-seated problem. Silently looking on may be used simply for

Figure 2 Teacher behaviour continuum

| Silently looking on | Non-directive statements | Questions | Directive statements | Modelling | Reinforcement | Physical intervention and isolation |

Source: from Wolfgang and Glickman (1986)

observation and collecting information without any attempt at changing behaviour, or the teacher's look may contain a signal intended to intimate that the teacher is aware of what is happening. Planned ignoring, signal interference and proximity control are the terms favoured by Redl and Wineman to describe some of the least interventionist responses which teachers will make to misbehaviour. They may plan to deliberately ignore it on the premise that provocative behaviour will extinguish itself if not successful in attracting attention. If this does not happen then a signal intended to block or interfere with the misbehaviour will be sent by a clear gesture of awareness through eye contact or from an admonitory shake of the head. If that signal does not deter the misbehaviour then the teacher may move close to the source of trouble in the hope that physical proximity will in itself provide a source of protection and reorientation.

If these non-verbal behaviours have failed to deter misbehaviour then verbal intervention through non-directive statements, questions and directive statements will reflect progression along the continuum. Examples given by Wolfgang and Glickman range from the non-directive, 'I saw you throw the book', through questioning, 'Why are you doing that?' to the directive 'Don't do that again!' But progression might also involve various techniques, described by Redl and Wineman, such as interest boosting and hurdle help designed to refocus attention on the task in hand, offering assistance on the assumption that any problems are to do with academic difficulty, rather than confrontation over the misbehaviour itself.

Modelling and reinforcement are used by teachers to demonstrate and to reward appropriate behaviours and physical intervention and isolation used to restrain and punish behaviours perceived as intolerable. Once more, a similar progression is evident in the techniques preferred by Redl and Wineman, including what they describe as 'hypodermic affection', an injection of praise or personal regard and 'antiseptic bouncing', the brisk and unemotional removal of a pupil from a problem situation.

Another helpful perspective on individual mediation or modification is provided by the concept of an escalation–

detonation staircase (Smith and Laslett, 1993) in which a confrontation between teacher and pupil can be seen as a series of steps mounting from initial friction towards an eventual explosion of animosity and possibly physical violence. As the responsible adult, the teacher should be able to exercise control of the situation by stopping further progress up the staircase by distraction, defusion or simply declining further participation in a dispute, postponing its resolution to a more propitious time. This is not an abdication of authority but an illustration of the point that assertive teaching does not need to be aggressive teaching. Rather than angrily taking the bait offered by disruptive behaviour teachers can calmly restate rules and remind pupils about routines: 'Remember, don't call out, put your hand up and wait your turn, that's the rule.' Distraction through questions about work, or defusion through a humorous response to a potentially challenging behaviour, will also provide a better model of mature self-control than increasingly angry and immature attempts to win an argument by talking down or shouting down an opponent.

As can be seen from their diagram (Figure 2), Wolfgang and Glickman plot a likely association between beliefs on dis- cipline and techniques for individual mediation through counselling and guidance or modification of conduct through confronting problems, agreeing plans for change and using systematic rewards and punishments to shape behaviour.

Within the Relationship–Listening approach, which seeks to give the pupil power and responsibility for his or her own behaviour, Teacher Effectiveness Training recommended by Gordon (1974) puts Rogerian theory into practice through 'active listening' reflecting back pupil feelings through summarising their perceptions and prompting more effective communication through supportive 'door opener' questions. Central to this approach is the issue of 'ownership' of problems and if the teacher clearly 'owns' the problem because of the effect of behaviour then the teacher's need is expressed through an 'I' message. Thus a pupil might not be reprimanded for calling out but told by the teacher that 'I cannot hear other children, if everyone talks at once.' Used together, 'active listening' and 'I' messages help the resolution of conflict through a 'no lose' process in which teacher and pupil identify each other's needs and jointly evolve a plan for solving the problem which is acceptable to both of them.

Other Relationship–Listening approaches analysed by Wolfgang and Glickman are Transactional Analysis (Berne, 1964; Harris, 1969) and Values Clarification (Raths, Harmin and Simon, 1966) where, in each case, the teacher helps a pupil analyse his or her own behaviour or values, whilst avoiding overt or covert direction on the assumption that misbehaviour results from misinterpretation which blocks rational thought and that once such obstacles are removed, the individual's innate capacity for being rational will be expressed.

In contrast the Confronting–Contracting school exemplified by Dreikurs (1968) and Glasser (1975) emphasise a more active and directive involvement for the teacher. Dreikurs advances a social theory, drawn from the work of Alfred Adler, which explains misbehaviour in terms of responses to failure to gain social acceptance through normal interaction, leading to annoying, destructive, hostile or helpless behaviours. Like the Relationship–Listener the teacher seeks to deal with the pupil's misinterpretation of a situation and develop more appropriate ways of getting along with other people. However, Dreikurs advocates more active intervention from the teacher through questioning and directive statements, designed to uncover and confront the goals of misbehaviour, and through arranging 'logical consequences', so that pupils are required to clear up any mess they make or stay in at playtime to finish work not completed during a lesson.

As its name suggests, Reality Therapy emphasises the importance of drawing pupils' attention to the boundaries of acceptable behaviour within society (Glasser, 1969, 1975). Inappropriate behaviour is seen merely as a way of escaping from the real world and people behaving in this way should be confronted with the consequences of their actions and pressed for a commitment to a plan for changing them. In this Confronting–Contracting approach questions and directive statements demand explanations and clearly stated explanations: 'What are you doing . . . you are breaking the rules and therefore cannot be part of the group . . . What are you going to do about it?' These questions are pursued through class meetings as well as in individual discussions used to elicit a realistic plan for changing behaviour which then becomes a contract for future interaction.

The rationale for what Wolfgang and Glickman describe as the Rules/Reward–Punishment school of beliefs on discipline is derived from the view of behaviourist psychologists that all behaviour is learned through an association between actions and their consequences. From this perspective, teachers have the power and responsibility to shape pupil behaviour through arranging outcomes which reward appropriate behaviour and, if necessary, punish inappropriate behaviour. Teachers set rules which define what is appropriate behaviour, provide rewards which reinforce and increase such behaviour and arrange unpleasant consequences to punish and reduce undesirable behaviour.

Reinforcement may take the form of direct tangible reward such as sweets; rewarding events such as extra time for play; token reinforcers such as points or stars to be later exchanged for one of the above, or simply social approval or praise. Thus earlier stages in the teacher behaviour continuum might be used to gather information about behaviour through observation, or elicit information about what will be effective reinforcement through questioning. In recent years behaviourist psychology has shown an increased interest in taking account of antecedents as well as consequences of behaviour (e.g. see Chapter 4 on the behavioural interactionist perspective suggested by Wheldall and Glynn, 1989) and given more consideration to motivation as well as directly observable behaviour (Walker, 1984). This has been reflected in a growing concern for what Bull and Solity (1987) call 'setting events', examining physical, social and educational factors in the classroom environment such as seating arrangements, group size and suitability of learning tasks, for their effect upon behaviour.

Whilst most behaviourist approaches emphasise positive reinforcement and turn to punishment reluctantly as a last resort, physical intervention and isolation has a more central role in the Assertive Teaching or Assertive Discipline model (Canter and Canter, 1976) which draws together various disciplinary measures used by teachers to establish their 'right to teach' and pupils' 'right to learn'. Bush and Hill (1993) describe its application in a special school for boys with emotional and behavioural difficulties. Rules are specified and, if transgressed, a hierarchy of consequences will follow. These range from merely recording a failure to obey and the name of the offender, through short detentions at breaktime, lunchtime and after school.

In mainstream schools, there may be a more extensive range of sanctions applied as part of a discipline plan, which ought always to include clear warning signals and an opportunity to choose to conform to established rules, or to continue to behave in a way which pupils know will lead to the application of sanctions in the form of loss of privilege, detention, isolation, report to senior teacher, complaint to parents and eventually removal and exclusion from school. It is essential that assertion is not confused with aggression, as Rogers (1991) puts it: 'assertion is distinguished between aggression and hostility on the one hand, and passivity and capitulating to student demands on the other'.

Assertive teaching is decisive not destructive, it is about teachers stating their needs, without demeaning or disparaging the needs of pupils. It is about encouraging compliance with rules which are there for the benefit of all, not about winning personal battles or showing who is boss. The teacher in the case study in Chapter 5 may intend to be assertive but gets drawn into a confrontation in which aggression is met with counter-aggression and the escalation–detonation staircase is rapidly mounted. One evident advantage of Canter's model is the extra steps it builds into the escalation–detonation staircase, and the additional opportunities it gives for participants to pause, rethink and possibly reframe the situation before proceeding further up the staircase. Provided that, as Rogers insists, rules are agreed to be fair and arrived at through discussion, which places them in a wider context of rights and responsibilities, so that there is a sense of ownership for pupils as well as teachers, and given that, as Bush and Hill report, there is an equally clear and positive set of rewards as well as sanctions, then this approach has much to offer; but with assertive discipline, as with any system of classroom management, continued success demands constant monitoring.

MONITORING SCHOOL POLICY

Policies involving sanctions such as those described above require agreement and planning with colleagues. Indeed, all schools will have devised some procedures for dealing with severely challenging behaviour but there may be a tendency to confuse discipline policy with punishment policy. Good discipline is not simply about maintaining order and dealing with transgressions of a formal code of regulations. An effective monitoring of school policy on discipline and behaviour should begin from the starting point identified by Stone (1990 p. 109): 'Where the school is now, what is working well, what areas need attention and how that attention is given. '

This can raise questions about whether interactions between staff, as well as interactions with pupils, promote an affirmative approach to management skills in classroom organisation and lesson presentation; about whether supportive mediation is available through counselling and guidance, and whether the school does have positive programmes for modifying inappropriate behaviour. The answers to these questions should provide an opportunity for staff to discuss rules, routines and beliefs about discipline.

For example, most schools and teachers will claim to follow an eclectic approach to discipline rather than total adherence to one of the three approaches described by Wolfgang and Glickman. Few schools, however, will have actually used such a conceptual framework to explore whether a change in approach may be useful with particular pupils. Using the concept of the continuum of teacher behaviour, a teacher finding that Relationship–Listening is not working might be encouraged to try the Confronting–Contracting approach and, if that does not work, to move on again to the Rules/Rewards–Punishment approach. Alternatively, the reasons for lack of conformity to existing rules, or confrontations over the applications of rewards and sanctions, might be fruitfully explored through non-directive counselling, which might then provide the chance to develop an individual plan for improvement.

The capacity to 'gear shift' up and down the teacher behaviour continuum is discussed by Wolfgang and Glickman in relation to individual teaching plans but it offers an equally valid construct for institutional planning. It also offers a helpful structure for applying the ecosystemic approach because it can be used to suggest possible points for changing perspectives for teacher and pupil.

In a broader sense, monitoring should review aspects of interactions within schools which reflect three key features of the ethos of successful schools: positive expectations, good models of behaviour and effective feedback on conduct (Smith, 1991), which together might be described as 'affirmative teaching' because they define the ways in which teachers affirm their belief in pupils' capacity to learn and change, and affirm their confidence in their ability to teach and help them.

Positive expectations for all pupils are conveyed through providing an inclusive curriculum, which genuinely seeks to give all pupils their entitlement to the National Curriculum, whilst differentiating tasks through varied styles of lesson delivery and adaptations of response which take account of individual levels of ability. The apparent lack of relevance of some learning experiences will inevitably increase the likelihood of disaffection. In this regard, innovations in courses in secondary schools with an emphasis on coursework, shorter modules or units which gain credit towards qualifications, personal profiles and records of achievement can all help retain the interest and enthusiasm of youngsters too easily deterred by traditional examination systems.

Teachers themselves can offer pupils good models of behaviour. Charlton and David (1989) suggest that pupils learn from teachers in the manner in which they show respect for others by readiness to listen and refrain from harsh, destructive criticism, the way in which they are sensitive to anxieties and willing to help overcome them and their ability to control their own emotions. Gray and Richer (1988) argue that disruptive behaviour often arises from pupil insecurity. To reduce this possibility, school policy should provide opportunities for staff to meet to review, and reach a consensus sufficient to establish, a predictable pattern of consistent teacher behaviour with regard to rules and work procedures.

Effective feedback on conduct should be ensured by further policy agreement by staff about rules and routines which are rational and reasonable, about differentiating tasks so that all pupils have a prospect of achieving success, and about marking which is frequent and constructive. Through regular opportunity to review and contribute to such discussions, staff should enjoy a real sense of 'ownership' of the system rather than mere compliance with it. How much better yet if this can be extended to pupils through involving them in such discussions?

Other aspects of giving effective feedback involve recognition for pupils as individuals and providing additional support where difficulties are experienced. Monitoring such interactions should involve senior staff in helping junior colleagues develop and experiment with varied teaching styles and classroom layout and design. This may best be achieved through team teaching, which is also nowadays the most usual way for providing support for pupils with learning difficulties in mainstream classes. This collegial or collaborative approach aims to share skills and expertise so that all teachers gain confidence in adapting methods and materials to meet a range of individual teaching needs for pupils with diverse levels of ability. Monitoring classroom management is part of a wider process of institutional change, necessary to ensure and maintain school effectiveness, and further consideration is given to this topic in Chapter 9.

Certain constructs have been used in this chapter to suggest a particular conceptual framework for establishing links between theory and practice in relation to classroom management. It is not suggested that this is the only, or necessarily the best, framework, but it is argued that unless some attempt is made to provide some underpinning from a theoretical rationale, effective classroom management can be too easily dismissed as a function of individual charisma, which someone either has or has not got, rather than a professional skill which can be acquired, developed and improved.

Part III

SOLUTIONS IN PRACTICE

OVERVIEW

Earlier, in Chapter 2, our description of educational responses to emotional and behavioural difficulties considered a variety of different approaches and concluded with the view that successful schools and units should be open to the process of institutional change. In this part of the book, we use two case studies as illustrative examples of the development and application of school policies for meeting the special needs of pupils with emotional and behavioural difficulties. One study looks at the role of the special school and reflects on the value of special schools or units, and the opportunities which they can provide for taking account of pupils' perceptions of themselves and their situations and responding to them in ways not easily available in other educational settings. The second study shows what can be achieved by a mainstream school in developing a whole school policy for dealing with behaviour problems. Each study highlights the importance of consultation and evaluation procedures. Our final chapter draws together advice on how schools can systematically make use of a wide range of possible solutions to emotional and behavioural difficulties, as an integral part of school development planning.

Based on studies in two residential schools, Chapter 7 identifies three critical features which residential special schools may offer to their pupils: *respite* from negative environmental influences, good interpersonal *relationships* with staff and fresh opportunities for personal achievement leading to *re-signification* of themselves with a more positive identity and self-image. Day special schools and units may also to some extent offer similar chances for a break from experiences which reinforce feelings of inadequacy and low self-esteem. Respite from the distress caused by adverse pressures from unhappy family circumstances, antagonistic schools and anti-social peer groups can offer the space and time to build new and more trusting relationships with staff whose training and experience enable them to offer supportive counselling and arrange opportunities for success, which help pupils see themselves in a more favourable light.

The next chapter, again based on an empirical study, illustrates how ordinary schools, too, can utilise the concepts of respite, relationships and re-signification in organising policies for behaviour, discipline and pastoral care. This chapter describes one school's successful transition from a situation characterised by disaffection and low morale to one characterised by confidence and self-respect. In this school, emotional and behavioural difficulties are seen within a whole school context, in which all aspects of the school's functioning as a community impinge on the well-being of pupils. This example may point the way for other mainstream schools to become more special in their response to individual needs, through strong leadership, consultation and effective communication.

In our last chapter, we turn to broader issues of school effectiveness. We suggest ways in which other schools may emulate the successes recorded by the research studies reported in Chapters 7 and 8 and we look at how schools might use the range of possible solutions suggested in this book. This chapter begins by reviewing the lessons to be learnt from the wide range of research, which shows the powerful influence which schools do have. We examine the conclusions which have been drawn about why some schools, working with pupils from similar backgrounds, are more effective than others in producing better academic results with fewer behavioural problems. This involves consideration of concepts such as 'ethos' and 'incorporation' and their implications for helping pupils with emotional and behavioural difficulties.

Finally, we consider the process of institutional change with particular regard to the effect of recent educational reforms. We suggest ways in which schools can monitor their own performance in using the range of possible solutions to problems presented by emotional and behavioural difficulties as part of their school development plan.

7

THE VALUE OF THE
SPECIAL SCHOOL OR
UNIT

This chapter is based on a study (Cooper, 1989, 1993) that was carried out in 1985 in two residential schools for boys with emotional and behavioural difficulties. The study set out to answer the question: 'What are the effects of residential schooling on pupils with emotional and behavioural difficulties?' The research methods involved participant observation, semi-structured, 'informant' style (see Powney and Watts, 1987) interviews with pupils, and staff (though the staff data is not reported here), as well as questionnaires. The questionnaires were designed to test the generalisability across the full pupil populations of both schools, of hypotheses generated from interviews with 24 pupils. Of particular interest were the pupils' perceptions of the nature and effects of their experience. The study did not seek to establish an objective measure of 'effects', but rather took the view that, by concentrating on the pupils' perceptions of 'effects', pupils would be encouraged to relate their experience of schooling to their actual behaviour and attitudes. In this way the researcher was able to uncover evidence which is central to the aims of school effectiveness research (see Chapter 9). In existing research, such connections can only be made on an inferential basis, owing to the absence of qualitative data of the type gathered in this study.

These pupils' accounts advance our understanding of school effectiveness by showing us how these pupils perceive aspects of their school experience, and how they relate these perceptions to their own behaviour. Of particular interest is how this diverse group of 77 boys (aged 14–19) produces a range of accounts which indicate a consensus of values with regard to the desirable and undesirable qualities of schools and how they believe these to influence their behaviour. Of further interest is the way in which these qualities can be related to school effectiveness research findings.

A common thread running through the accounts of these pupils is an indication of the importance of three critical features, which have a powerful influence on the pupils' views of schooling, depending on their presence or absence. These qualities are:

- *respite* from negative environmental influences, in the form of adverse family circumstances, a negative experience of schooling, or problems associated with membership of a delinquescent peer group;
- good quality interpersonal *relationships* with school staff, and other significant persons in their lives;
- availability of *opportunities* for personal achievement and positive recognition in a supportive yet challenging environment.

These qualities are associated to different degrees with individual pupils' perceptions of the outcomes they have experienced, and continue to experience, in their residential schools.

Not surprisingly, given the boys' placement in residential schools for pupils with emotional and behavioural difficulties, these boys tend to be preoccupied with the social and interpersonal aspects of schooling and their own emotional and behavioural development. Strongest among the impressions conveyed by the boys is a sense of personal achievement. All but two out of 24 of the boys interviewed felt that they had arrived at the residential schools with highly negative images of themselves which, in the course of their stay at the schools, had been reshaped to the extent that they now defined themselves in positive terms and had a clear sense of their own self-worth. Recurrent aspects of this development claimed by pupils are:

- mastery of behavioural and emotional problems, and an improved sense of self-control;
- mastery of particular social skills;
- improved ability to engage in constructive reflection on their actions;
- mastery of practical and academic skills.

These outcomes are directly related by these pupils to the three qualities of: respite, relationships and opportunities (see above). Each of these categories will now be exemplified in a little more detail, though a more thorough account can be found in Cooper (1989, 1993).

RESPITE

The pinpointing of 'respite' as an important quality arises from the boys' repeated references to the value they place on being temporarily removed from stressful home situations (which might involve family discord, peer group problems or school-based difficulties). The residential environment was felt by the boys to provide a setting which gave them time to reflect on these problematic circumstances in an atmosphere of relative calm.

Circumstances which the boys experienced in their family settings, and which they describe as adverse, can be summarised under the headings of:

- economic and social disadvantage;
- severe emotional tension and discord within family;
- the presence of delinquescent influences within the family.

Problems of economic and social disadvantage include: low income, poor living conditions, large family size and parental absence. Emotional tension and discord within the family are exemplified by: discord and quarrelling between parents, between parents (or step parent) and children, among siblings, and violence between parents (or step parent) and children. Delinquescent influences are described in terms of: parental or sibling involvement in delinquent activities, parental or sibling absence as a result of penal detention. Of particular interest is the fact that this range of problems covers a wide range of factors which have been identified in large sample research and surveys as being statistically associated with childhood deviance (West and Farrington, 1973; Millham *et al.*, 1975; Rutter, 1975; Hoghughi, 1978; Millham *et al.*, 1978; Rutter and Giller, 1983; Reid, 1985).

It is important to note that, where they are mentioned, these circumstances are often described as providing a source of stress and discomfort to the boy concerned: they are seen as difficulties by the boys themselves. Thus, for example, one boy describes feelings of distress as a result of his siblings having been dispersed as a result of being taken into local authority care, and describes the strain that his visits home from residential school had placed on his relationship with his mother, owing to the difficulties she had in coping alone with a large number of young children.

School problems prior to placement in the residential school, that are identified by the residential school boys, tend to focus on:

- unsatisfactory staff–pupil relationships;
- inconsistent and unfair treatment of pupils by staff;
- lack of academic and personal support for pupils from staff;
- intolerable institutional demands of some schools.

In common with other studies reporting the perceptions of disaffected school pupils (e.g. Rosser and Harré, 1976; Woods, 1979, 1990b; Tattum, 1982), the boys in the present study often account for their dissatisfaction with schooling in terms of their feelings of alienation. These boys often describe a relationship of antipathy between them and their former schools. They complain of being wrongly accused of misdemeanours and often recurrent phrases in the pupil interviews refer to their being 'chucked out', 'thrown out', 'put away'. Typical responses include:

> You didn't know them [teachers in the comprehensive school] that well. You're only getting about 35 minutes a day with them, with everyone else. I don't think they cared. They said, 'It's your life. It's up to you. You do what you like.'
>
> (14-year-old boy)

> Teachers in comprehensives are all stuck up. Here [at the residential school] they're flexible. Staff are more friendly. You can call them by their first names and everything. Staff will give you more time, if you want to talk to them. Charlie [a teacher] will stay with you, even if he's off duty, until it [i.e. a personal problem] is sorted out. They have more time for you.
>
> (14-year-old boy)

[The staff at this school are] a lot better. They're more like people! When I was at Rushforth [day special school], they were more like robots really. You do something wrong, the first thing they do is grab 'em and stick 'em in a room, and just lock them up!

(13-year-old boy)

The third area of difficulty relates to pupils' home-based peer group associations. A common difficulty for some of these boys was a sense of being caught in a web of delinquescence, both in and out of their home-based schools. This accords well with the findings of other researchers who have described the ways in which children and young people who occupy low 'deprived of status' positions in the formal hierarchy of schools often form associations with peers of similar status, and develop a counter-culture which simultaneously rejects the values of the formal school culture, and provides opportunities for high status which depend on this contrary set of values (Hargreaves, 1967; Rutter and Giller, 1983; Coleman and Hendry, 1990).

Other problems relating to peer group factors include difficulties associated with marginal status. Several pupils describe their feelings of frustration and humiliation in face of mockery from peers because of their poor educational performance. These feelings are often also associated with behaviour designed to curry favour with peers. One 13-year-old boy claims:

They [his classmates] used to dare me to do things. Like shout things out. I did [. . .] I didn't care. It was a laugh! We used to have a good laugh [. . .] I used to get told off. It was just having a laugh.

Other pupils describe their almost total withdrawal from contact with peers, through school refusal.

It is important to recognise that this range of problems is also reflected in the research literature on deviant and disturbed young people (West and Farrington, 1973; Dunlop, 1974; Pringle, 1975; Hoghughi, 1978; Tattum, 1982; Rutter and Giller, 1983). Whilst few pupils experience all of these problems (though some do), all of the interviewees experienced one or more of them. Particularly prominent were school and family problems. Whilst it would be simplistic to think of these problems as causes of emotional and behavioural difficulties, it seems to be the case that, for these pupils, the experience of having to cope with difficult circumstances such as these seemed to occupy their energies to the exclusion of all else. And often, although the boys were seen by others as being a source of some of these problems, the boys felt themselves to be powerless (though, ironically, rarely blameless) to change their behaviour. The respite provided by the residential situation enabled many of these boys to simply break this vicious cycle of distress. Respite, in itself, is for these pupils a necessary starting point for their positive development, since it gives them relief from circumstances which maintain their problems.

RELATIONSHIPS

On the basis of pupils' perceptions, staff–pupil relationships in the residential schools can be characterised in the following terms:

- pupils believe staff to be caring, and an atmosphere of mutual trust prevails;
- pupils tend to have preferred members of staff in whom they confide and place particular trust;
- relationships among pupils tend to reflect the positive values identified in staff–pupil relationships, to the extent that some pupils provide their own support networks and engage in informal peer counselling;
- staff–pupil relationships are seen as central to the therapeutic purpose of the schools, as identified by staff, and the therapeutic effect of the schools, as experienced by pupils;
- by and large, pupils value most highly those staff who they feel are prepared to listen to them and be sympathetic, and are less inclined to resist these staff when they make demands on them. Staff who are perceived to be uncaring are inclined to be the focus for resistance.

Relationships of high quality with staff and fellow pupils in the residential community contribute to the development of more positive self-images, by giving pupils a sense of being valued and cared for by significant others, whom they have learned to trust. In response to a questionnaire based on interview responses over 80 per cent of the total pupil population in both schools agreed with the following statements:

- Pupils here like this school because the teachers here give them more help with their schoolwork than teachers in ordinary schools.
- Pupils here like this school because the staff here listen to pupils, when pupils want to talk to them.
- The staff here help pupils if they have a personal problem.
- The staff here give pupils more personal attention than staff in ordinary schools.

Typical interview responses are:

There was an incident a couple of weeks ago, where I was piling my plate with food, cos I was starving [. . .]. Charlie [a teacher] said, 'Leave enough for everyone else!' And with that I just slammed my knife and fork down and walked out! He came after me, after about 15 minutes, when I'd had a good cry in the bathroom, and said, 'Try not to worry about what's happening.' I can't remember what he said now, but he gave me new ideas.

The staff here are more prepared to sit down and talk to you, and talk your problems out. There was one member of staff, Fiona, she's left. She used to remind me of my sister and that, cos she was the same age as my sister and everything. I used to be able, if I'd got any problems to talk to her.

Yes, the staff here do care, especially 'Mo' [deputy head teacher], Hamish [head of care], and Charlie [. . .]. He's [Charlie] a really good talker; he can really talk to you and let you know what's happening. And he gives you new ideas [. . .] when he's talking to you about your problems.

Before I came here, I never used to talk to anyone about my problems [. . .]. I used to say nothing to no-one, when I had a problem. [Now] I talk to anyone about my problems..

I think he's [teacher] helped me quite a bit. He's helped me with my work; talked to me quite a bit. Like I never used to like going out anywhere, to do anything. Now I feel quite happy to go to snooker clubs. John [the teacher] takes quite

143

a few of us there. We save our pocket money from the weekend to go there.

[. . .] they've [the staff] helped me [. . .]. [I've talked about] problems at home. They give me advice sometimes, when they can help me [. . .]

The school's put me in a different way, y'know. It's made me look at things different. [. . .] I didn't get on with my mum and brothers, and I used to argue with my mum. That's just stopped now. There's things I wouldn't do, like say I have a little argument with my mum, I'll say sorry to her after. That's something I wouldn't ever thought of doing when I was at home before.

High quality staff–pupil relationships are perhaps the single most important mechanism at work in these schools, since it is through the experience of being valued in significant relationships that pupils are exposed to an image of themselves as worthy and valuable human beings. Furthermore, they provide pupils with a sense of security and support, which forms an essential basis from which they can address personal challenges.

OPPORTUNITIES

The term 'signification' has been employed by Hargreaves *et al.* (1975) to describe a key component of the process by which pupils come to be labelled as 'deviant'. The term is used by Matza (1976) to describe the point at which an individual's persona comes to be identified with a particular form of deviance. It is the process by which a pupil becomes objectified as a 'yob', 'truant' or 'bully', as opposed to being seen simply as a pupil who sometimes behaves like a 'yob', 'truant' or 'bully'. Positive signification or re-signification (Cooper, 1989, 1993), it is suggested, occurs when the pupil comes to be labelled with a positive identity to replace a deviant identity. The effect of such labelling is to set in motion a self-fulfilling prophecy, whereby people judge only that behaviour which accords with the label as typical of the individual, and the labelled individual comes to develop a self-image that is in keeping with the label. Re-signification, it is argued, describes the process that many of the boys in this study are undergoing in their residential schools. Re-signification involves the development of new and positive identities as a consequence of relationships and experiences which undermine the pupils' negative self-image, by revealing evidence of desirable, and positive, qualities of self.

Re-signification is achieved through the availability in these two residential schools of opportunities for pupils to take on new challenges, learn new skills, develop a deeper knowledge of themselves, and move towards a more positive acceptance of themselves. To succeed this process depends upon the supportive structure of good staff–pupil relationships (see above) and a secure environment, as well as the provision of carefully controlled but challenging situations, in which effort and success are rewarded, and community involvement is encouraged, acknowledged and rewarded. In its early stages, re-signification involves the highlighting and rewarding of positive attributes that the pupils already possess. For its success, however, it has to be progressive, providing an impetus to pupils to take on new challenges.

In the residential school, opportunities of the following type were evident:

- pupil participation in the organisation and running of the schools;
- clear and formally defined areas of pupil autonomy;
- recognition for success and in a wide range of areas (including academic, practical, social and personal) acknowledged through the formal privilege and status system;
- the availability of channels for pupils to air their personal concerns and grievances effectively.

In both schools, pupils received recognition and rewards for positive academic, emotional and behavioural progress. The range of possible rewards was wide, covering everything from sweets or additional pocket money to additional home visits, and the bestowal of specific responsibilities. An important aspect of the reward structure appears to have been its public nature. In both schools, pupils who were believed to have 'done well' were rewarded publicly in meetings and assemblies. Similarly, pupils' classwork was often displayed, and it was not unusual for pupils in both schools to be given permission to take examples of their good work to chosen members of staff for their approval during class time.

Pupils' involvement in the running of their schools was facilitated through the use of group meetings with staff and pupils, and through regular formal and informal consultation between staff and pupils. Pupils in both schools believed that they could have an influence on the way in which their schools were run, and their personal circumstances, through one or other of these channels. In a narrower sense, pupils exercised a degree of autonomy over their living conditions, being permitted to decorate their bedrooms, and being consulted by staff about their personal and group requirements. As pupils got older, the degree of autonomy increased, with the oldest pupils in both schools occupying self-contained accommodation.

LEARNING FROM THE PUPIL PERSPECTIVE

It is clear from this and other studies (e.g. Hargreaves, 1967; Hargreaves *et al.*, 1975; Rosser and Harré, 1976; Ball, 1981; Tattum, 1982; Schostak, 1983; Cronk, 1987; Woods, 1990b), that we can learn a great deal from studying the pupil perspective on schooling. From the study discussed above, we have learned about the importance that a group of pupils labelled as having emotional and behavioural difficulties attach to environmental influences. The claims of these pupils accord well with the findings of researchers who have explored the social and psychological correlates of deviance (see above). Their perceptions of the negative aspects of schooling relate well to earlier studies of pupils' perceptions (e.g. Rosser and Harré, 1976; Tattum, 1982; Schostak, 1983; Woods, 1990b) in that it is consistently asserted that school deviance is often experienced by its perpetrators as a reasonable response to intolerable circumstances. The present study, however, takes us a step further, in that it begins to give some indication of the kinds of situations and mechanisms that might work to halt the development of deviant careers and re-route pupils on to more constructive paths. This study, therefore, can be related to Cronk's (1987), because of the evidence it presents of the power of supportive social and interpersonal relationships between staff and pupils to achieve these desirable ends. The present study goes further still, in revealing pupils' views of the institutional arrangements which they believe facilitate the positive outcomes they experience, and in so doing shows us how valuable such data might be in school evaluation programmes.

From these pupils' views we can see the way in which the residential school community can be seen to be a therapeutic tool, very much in the mould of the early pioneer establishments in this field (Bettelheim, 1950; Bridgeland, 1971). Much of what these schools achieve is based on a recognition of the way in which everyday social and interpersonal experiences can affect the social and emotional development of individuals, and the belief that pupils' emotional adjustment and behaviour can be influenced by direct manipulation of environmental influences. As will be seen in Chapter 9, these values are highly compatible with the findings of the school effectiveness researchers and begin to suggest possible explanatory theories. In the following chapter, we will examine the ways in which these insights have been put to practical use in an English comprehensive school.

8

MAKING THE ORDINARY SCHOOL SPECIAL

In this chapter consideration will be given to one school and its attempt to tackle the problem of disaffection and low attainment among its pupils. The school concerned is a real comprehensive school, which for the purposes of this book has been fictitiously named 'the Valley School'. (Certain other alterations have also been made in order to protect the privacy of the school, its parents, pupils, teachers and local authority.) The two most important features of this chapter are: (i) the way in which the three concepts of respite, relationships and positive-signification (opportunities), which were generated in the study of the residential pupils' perceptions (Chapter 7), can be shown to provide useful structures for organising our thinking about this school's approach to enhancing its effectiveness; and (ii) indications that are given as to the ways in which developments and changes within the school were managed. The data on which this section is based were collected in a series of interviews with staff (including the head teacher) and pupils at the school. The aim of this chapter is to describe one school's practical experience of a successful transition from a situation in which pupils and staff were disaffected and poorly motivated, to one where the consensus is that the school has improved its effectiveness, and where there is a shared confidence among the staff that the school has the means to further improve its effectiveness. It is suggested that this approach to the concept of school effectiveness, which places stronger emphasis on the subjectivity of staff and pupils than conventional approaches, contributes a valuable perspective to the debate which is complementary to existing work in this area.

THE SCHOOL

The Valley School is a mixed comprehensive school for pupils between the ages of 13 and 18. The school is situated on the Valley corporation housing estate, on the outskirts of a medium-sized city in the English midlands. The school has an open entry 6th form which accounts for approximately 25 per cent of the school roll (in 1990/91). The school is also a regional centre for pupils with learning difficulties, catering for up to 40 pupils who are integrated into the mainstream of the school. The school is unique among its immediate neighbours, being the only non-selective school in the area.

The present head teacher, Ms Eileen Lincoln, found the school to be in a sorry state when she took over the headship in 1982. She describes a situation marked by:

- low staff morale;
- internal divisions among the staff;
- a highly coercive disciplinary regime;
- high levels of indiscipline, disruption and suspensions/ exclusions;
- high levels of truancy;
- poor examination results;
- an inappropriate curriculum;
- high levels of pupil delinquency;
- low self-esteem among pupils;
- vandalised, and graffiti-scarred, school buildings.

Public examination results for the year 1985/86 were extremely poor, with less than 10 per cent of pupils entered for GCSE or equivalent exams achieving a C grade or better. Similarly, the high level of pupil delinquency was reflected in the fact that between 10 and 20 pupils a year were subject to criminal prose-cution between 1980 and 1984. She describes the state of pupil morale in the following terms:

> Now the pupils: when I came there was little self-respect. Damaged buildings; graffitied buildings. You asked them what they thought of their school – I'd been for many years [a deputy head] in a super school, and to hear pupils run their school down, and run their teachers down, as they did here, was a real eye-opener. I couldn't believe it. And it

made me very sad, because I'd been used to children being really proud of their school, and wanting to be at school; enjoying school.

The staff were in a similar state:

They [the staff] knew the curriculum was wrong, but they didn't know how to put it right. [. . .] They could see that what they were doing was not successful. Nobody comes into work to do a bad job, but they were going home feeling very dissatisfied with what they had done, because they were not winning.

Interviewer: Was that because of poor exam results?

Ms Lincoln: Disruption in the classroom. They believed you didn't really look for results in a comprehensive school. Because they were so indoctrinated against it, by what happened locally. Their expectations were very low.

Ms Lincoln places much blame for the staff and pupil attitudes on to the local political climate in education. She believes that the previous head teacher, placed in the invidious position of having to compete with local grammar schools, developed a school ethos which attempted to 'ape the grammar schools'. Major consequences of this were the imposition of an inappropriate curriculum, and the failure to develop the necessary systems of social and academic support required by a comprehensive pupil population with more than its fair share of pupils considered to be 'less able'. Teachers and pupils were not giving themselves the opportunity to make the best of their situation, they were, rather, constantly setting themselves up to fail, academically and socially. Thus pupils arrived at the school at 13, having already failed to obtain grammar school places, only to face further failure, almost immediately. Ms Lincoln cites the example of modern languages:

[. . .] everybody coming into the school at 13 had to do two languages: French and Spanish. Now, that was because good grammar schools are known to offer two languages. But you had within that no special needs set up. So for some children English was already a foreign language. So you were saying not only are you going to fail at English, but we'll make darn sure you fail at French, and even more, you'll fail at Spanish too!

The school's response to such failure was to remove the pupils who were failing most conspicuously to more practically oriented subjects. This led to the situation whereby:

There was no balance and breadth in the options that pupils were steered into. There were quite a few who were doing no science at all [after year 9]; quite a few who were doing no humanities at all. And of course, as was usual at that time, many of the least able were doing everything that tired them out: metalwork, woodwork, tech. drawing, car maintenance and P.E.

Furthermore, there was a significant proportion (approximately 10 per cent) of the school population which was excluded from the existing curriculum; these included the 40 pupils in the Moderate Learning Difficulties (MLD) Unit, and a group of 25 non-statemented pupils, referred to as the Alternative Learning Programme (ALP) group, who had been excluded from mainstream classes for behavioural reasons. Both of these groups were physically segregated from their fellow pupils during class time and followed restricted curricula, taught by a limited range of staff.

Alongside these problems, the state of staff–pupil relationships was, in Ms Lincoln's words, 'not quite right'. Staff were authoritarian in their approach to relationships with pupils, tending to adopt coercive disciplinary strategies, and this engendered resentment among pupils and conflict between staff and pupils. For their part, the pupils had few opportunities for positive involvement in school life, with formal channels of communication between staff and pupils being almost entirely one way. Thus, because of the combination of an unsatisfactory curriculum, poor attainment levels, unsatisfactory staff–pupil relationships, and a negative public image, the experiences of being a pupil or teacher at the Valley were not happy ones; on the contrary, these experiences were marked by feelings of frustration and failure.

FACING THE PROBLEMS

Ms Lincoln was clear in her own mind about the kind of school of which she wanted to be Head:

> I believe deeply that if the curriculum is right, and the relationships are right, then everything else falls into place [...] you've got to have children wanting to come to school, no matter how bad things are at home, or no matter how unsuccessful they feel [...]. You've got to entice them to school, and let them see school as a way forward; an enjoyable place to be; something they're going to get something out of; and something that perhaps in many cases is going to help them forget the horrors that they live with at home: a sanctuary.

She was also clear about the fact that she would not be able to achieve these things single-handed. Not surprisingly, perhaps, the governing body of the school, which had appointed her, were highly supportive of her, and prepared to put their names to decisions which sometimes appeared risky and avant garde. As Ms Lincoln puts it:

> The governors were right behind me, in that we set out to be different: to be a good comprehensive school; a quality school. And they backed me all the way on that. Even to the extent that, one of the first things we did was to get rid of the traditional school uniform and tie. Because you know and I know that there's two ways of wearing a tie; one is: 'I'm proud of this school', and the other is down here, which says: 'Two fingers up to this place! I loathe it!' And they even backed me into going into schoolwear, rather than uniform, which was a very dicey move to make in an area which is so uniformed on the other side [i.e. in the selective schools]. But they backed me on that, and they wouldn't change it for the world now.

The staff, however, would require more careful handling, if Ms Lincoln were to achieve the ambitious aims which she had set for herself. Ms Lincoln realised that staff support would have to be earned:

153

The first thing you've got to do is build up your relationships with your staff, so they are not suspicious of you,
where they build up trust in you, and see you as an
individual who cares about them: be that about their
professional life, be that about their personal life. And in
return you expect the best out of them.

From the start, then, Ms Lincoln realised that she could not
change the Valley School single-handedly; she could only do so
with the co-operation of others, particularly the staff. The first
hurdle to be negotiated was a management structure which did
not encourage communication between staff and management.
Ms Lincoln's first step here was to expand the existing
management team of head teacher and two deputies to include
three senior teachers. This was intended to help bridge the gulf
between classroom teachers and management, and offer staff
more chance of rising through the ranks towards senior management positions. This important innovation was the first step
in increasing staff involvement in the decision-making process: a
development which was to be the foundation for the school's
future improvement.

The improvement programme initiated by Ms Lincoln and
her management team centred around a series of whole staff
meetings, which were termed 'workshops', which took place
once or twice a term. These workshops serve the dual function of
staff training and policy development. A key feature of these
meetings is staff participation. The workshops are each
organised around a question or problem which is of current
concern in the school. Topics so far covered include:

- What makes a good school?
- The role of the form tutor: healing the pastoral/academic
  divide.
- Devising a school environment development plan.
- Record keeping: what should records contain?
- Models of record keeping.
- 'What should be done if?' responding to problem behaviour
  in the school.
- Rewards for pupils.
- Public relations; the Valley School and the community.

The format of the meetings varies according to the topic, but the common pattern is for the meeting to commence with a presentation, in which a problem is stated and staff are briefed as to the task in hand. Staff then break into small discussion groups (six or seven to a group), where the outcomes of their talk are recorded. After the meeting these outcomes are collated by a member of the senior management team, and a report is prepared and distributed to staff. Topics for further meetings are often generated from this process, thus ensuring that the focus is kept on issues which are felt to be of general importance to staff. These workshops are often directed towards policy issues, and where policy decisions are required, these are made by the management team on the basis of consultation in workshops and reported in the workshop report.

The workshop approach combines many of the features which Lewis (1985), drawing on Organisational Development theory, sees as vital to effective communication within organisations:

1 the workshops create channels of communications between staff at all levels in the school hierarchy and, together with the recording and reporting procedures, this helps to enhance the *clarity of communication* among staff;

2 clarity of communication allows the *establishment of clear goals* which, because they are the subject of open scrutiny and debate, are felt to be under staff ownership;

3 the openness of the workshop programme allows *conflict* of perspective and opinion to be aired and dealt with constructively, thus avoiding the destructive effects of suppressed conflict;

4 the goal-directed small-group work which is central to the workshop programme enables the staff to utilise *group processes* in an effective way, as well as providing practice in the use of group work skills;

5 the sharing of concerns and perspectives fostered by the workshop programme allows common concerns to be brought to the fore, and for priorities for action to be set, thus facilitating *effective problem identification*, which is a prerequisite of *effective problem solving*;

6 finally, consultation and involvement aids *decision making* by

creating, among staff as a whole, a sense of ownership of, and commitment to, decisions that are made as a result of such processes.

Initially, the consultation programme was misinterpreted by some staff. In the written report of the first workshop (entitled: 'What makes a good school?') Ms Lincoln made the following comments, which highlight the more directive side of her management style:

Staff views were certainly divided as to the success of the consultation procedures within the school, according to the comments made. I must, however, make it clear: in any school where I am Head, decisions will be taken following consultation with you and after listening to a wide range of views. It will never be a participative form of government with the majority vote carrying the day or based on a Countersthorpe-type moot. The governors appointed me Head with full approval of my style of management; that's what they wanted and that's the way it will be. [. . .] Listen I will to your opinions, always, but the fact that you don't always like the final decisions taken does not mean you have not been consulted or that it was only lip service being paid! My accountability is not only to the staff but to the whole community of which members of staff are certainly an important part. Through more frequent staff meetings I will have more opportunity of giving you feedback on why particular decisions, popular and unpopular, have been made.

The important point to note here is the openness of the dialogue which takes place between the staff and management. Whilst staff consensus is not always the basis for decision making, staff views always contribute to decision making, sometimes in the sense that they indicate that a decision that the senior management feel to be necessary is unpopular. In such circumstances, the unpopularity of a decision is examined and attempts made to address staff concerns in the implementation of the decision. In this way, staff ownership of decisions is encouraged, even when the decision is not a popular one. A further means by which the consultation process was extended was through the introduction of annual 'Staff Development Interviews' in which members of the senior management team interview every member of staff individually, to discuss matters of professional development, and views of the way in which the school is developing.

CHANGING THE VALLEY SCHOOL

The workshops provided the springboard for many of the changes and innovations that were to shape the school after Ms Lincoln became Head. In this section some of these changes will be briefly considered, along with their implications for improving the effectiveness of the school.

What makes a good school?

The first staff workshop was entitled 'What makes a good school?' The outcomes of this workshop formed the basis for many of the changes which were to take place over the following years. This workshop presented the staff with three tasks:

1 to construct a list of qualities that characterises 'a good school';
2 to consider the ways in which the Valley School matched up to this list;
3 to make practical suggestions as to how the Valley School might be brought closer to the ideal espoused in (1).

The first task produced the following.

A good school is one where there is:

- a strong Head with a good sense of direction; obvious and effective leadership;
- pride in school;
- a good resourcing level;
- a caring community, where there is respect for people and property;
- a quiet environment;
- a desire to do well – a community where achievement in all spheres is encouraged;
- sensitivity with respect to the demands on staff in the management of change;

- a group of governors who are involved in the school;
- an established disciplinary framework, help and support for new, probationary and supply staff;
- effective communications;
- effort to cultivate a good public image;
- stability – traditional values;
- a climate of educational forward thinking and innovation;
- evidence of good exam results;
- a lack of graffiti, litter, damage;
- a clear and up-to-date policy about what the school is attempting to do; a set of clearly stated common goals;
- evidence of good working relationships with other schools;
- confidence that visitors can be taken to any part of the school at any time;
- an abundance of extra-curricular activities;
- a good atmosphere.

There are clear messages here about how the staff believe they should be led and how they think they should be treated. There is also concern for the quality of experience offered to pupils, and the need for a wide range of avenues to success for pupils. The third major area of concerns is the school's public image, and the belief that this should be a positive and attractive one.

Two additional lists of qualities produced at this workshop relate specifically to pupils and staff. The pupil list is as follows.

A good school is one where:

- pupils of all abilities are achieving set goals and achieving their potential;
- there is a good work ethic;
- pupils take responsibility for themselves;
- pupils have self-respect and respect for others;
- there is care taken of the environment, pride in the school and a sense of belonging and identity;
- there is a good range of sports, leisure and extra-curricular activities;
- pupils have sense of commitment and purpose;
- we [the staff] would be happy for our own and our friends' children to attend;

- pupils also behave well outside school;
- there are good sports results.

The staff list contains the following items.

A good school is one where:

- staff can practise their own specialities;
- staff are happy to work and morale is high;
- staff are professionals;
- staff are able to respond to pupils' individual needs;
- there is consistency and uniformity of standards, re behaviour and discipline;
- staff, including supply staff, are respected;
- staff work as a team without excessive hierarchical structure;
- staff have a commitment to providing a curriculum for the whole ability range, believing in equality of opportunity for pupils of all abilities, and where curriculum support is available to bring out the best in pupils;
- there are good relationships between staff and pupils.

These lists provide an important insight into the type of community this group of teachers aspires towards. The underlying message here is that a good school is one where pupils' needs and aspirations are catered for, where pupils are encouraged to feel a sense of commitment and belonging to their school, and also where schooling contributes to the development of self-esteem and pupils are proud to be associated with the school. Similarly, staff needs have to be recognised and circumstances created whereby these can be met. In a nutshell, a good school, according to these teachers, is one where staff and pupils coexist harmoniously, and share in the life of their school community, whilst enjoying the necessary levels of support which enable them to take full advantage of a wide range of opportunities designed to make the most of their needs and potentialities.

The scale of the ideals expressed in this first stage of the workshop was matched by the size of the gulf perceived to exist between these ideals and the reality of the Valley School. The range of shortcomings, identified by staff, include:

- the failure of the school to 'stretch' its most able pupils;
- the low self-esteem felt by many pupils;

- the poor public image/low public status of the school;
- the failure of a minority of pupils (20 per cent to 25 per cent) to conform to behavioural expectations;
- the lack of consistency among staff in their behavioural expectations of pupils;
- management ignore majority staff views without adequate explanation;
- realisation that the disciplinary approach to problem pupils is not always appropriate, but a lack of knowledge of how to cope with problems that may stem from pupils' personal difficulties;
- pressure, felt by staff, of current climate of change;
- lack of stability for pupils caused by internal changes (new Head and other staff changes) and externally [i.e. 1988 Education Reform Act] imposed changes.

In short, the staff felt the school to be failing in virtually all of the areas that had been identified in their considerations of what makes a good school: staff felt undervalued, there was a lack of consistency among staff, pupils were underachieving and misbehaving to a significant extent, and pupils and staff seemed subject to low morale and low self-esteem.

Understandably, there was less success in generating immediate solutions to these longstanding difficulties. However, in recognising and publicising them, the all important first step of identifying areas where improvement had to be made had been taken. Over the following months and years a succession of developments took place (and, at the time of writing, continue to take place), many of which can be seen as direct responses to problems identified in this first workshop. Brief consideration will now be given to some of the more significant developments that have taken place.

THE CURRICULUM

There was a general sense of despair among the staff about the curriculum, when Ms Lincoln became Head. It was clear from the poor examination results that pupils were not achieving well, and a poorly organised option system led to some pupils giving up science and humanities at the end of year 9. The least able pupils in the mainstream were sometimes finding their timetables unbalanced by the presence of too many practical and vocational subjects. Given the sense of despair and a lack of confidence among staff about how to alter this unsatisfactory situation, the management took a major lead in redesigning the curriculum. A deputy head was largely responsible for this task, though he carried this out in consultation with colleagues at all levels. An important first step was to consult staff in the development of a list of social, personal and academic aims for pupils at the school. The curriculum which was eventually put into place embodies many of the principles which run through staff thinking about the shortcomings of their school. Whereas the old curriculum was designed to ape that of the local grammar schools, the new curriculum addressed more directly the needs of the Valley pupils. The core curriculum of ten subjects reflects almost exactly the National Curriculum, and all pupils are required to take all of these subjects to GCSE (General Certificate of Secondary Education) level. In addition, at the end of year 9, pupils are required to choose an additional subject. There is also a range of 'top up' options for pupils with sufficient space on their timetables. The curriculum is strongly influenced by TVEI (Training and Vocational Education Initiative) thinking, carrying an emphasis on coursework and industrial/technical/ commercial studies and student-centred learning approaches, as well as the more traditional academic studies. Modular approaches are also favoured, and there is a strong emphasis placed on giving pupils first-hand experience of real life situations and opportunities to reflect on their own situations and environment. One subject on the core course is Community and Industrial Studies, which leads to the GCSE in Social Science. This course is based wholly on the study of the local community and its industry, and includes a two-week placement for each pupil with a local employer. At the time of writing the new curriculum was well under way at the Valley, and staff opinions were claimed by senior management to be very favourable towards it. Since then, of course, there have been government-sponsored changes in the balance between coursework and final examination at GCSE, which will inevitably influence the curriculum at the Valley. The impact of these and other changes is not known at the time of writing, but it seems fair to state that the current government's emphasis on examinations and pencil-and-paper testing is not likely to favour the kind of student-centred approach adopted at the school.

THE INTEGRATION OF PUPILS WITH SPECIAL EDUCATIONAL NEEDS AND THE CURRICULUM SUPPORT FACULTY

In 1984, when Ms Lincoln took over the headship of the Valley School, over 10 per cent of the school roll was permanently excluded from the mainstream curriculum. Forty pupils attended the regional Moderate Learning Difficulties (MLD) unit, which was attached to the school, but operated a completely self-contained curriculum, and a further 25 pupils, considered to have learning and/or behavioural difficulties, were placed in the Alternative Learning Programme (ALP) Group, and followed a discrete curriculum. When Ms Lincoln first raised the question of integration, she met with considerable staff opposition, from both mainstream and unit teachers. Mainstream staff felt themselves to lack the necessary skills for teaching pupils with learning difficulties, and the unit teachers felt they lacked skills appropriate to teaching mainstream classes. Although determined to achieve integration, Ms Lincoln and her management team realised that this could only be achieved with the support of the staff group.

In order to achieve this, a carefully staged integration programme was embarked upon, starting with attempts to win over staff to the principle of integration. First, it was pointed out to staff, in a series of meetings and through informal and formal contacts with staff, the ways in which an integration programme could be seen as a means of addressing certain sources of disquiet among staff, particularly the low status of pupils in the MLD unit, who were scorned and stigmatised by many mainstream pupils, as 'thickies' and 'dimbos'. Integration of these pupils, it was argued, would 'normalise' these pupils in the eyes of the mainstream pupils and so lessen the sense of stigma. Secondly, it was felt by staff that the ALP group represented an admission of failure. The ALP group was a source of shame within the school, that had to be kept out of the sight of visitors.

Once in this group, pupils tended to decline and take on the identity of 'no hopers'. Ms Lincoln was convinced that the lack of opportunity for legitimate success in the ALP group contributed to their worsening behaviour: 'It was little wonder that they weren't surviving: they'd failed so often, they'd turned to misbehaving to try and show themselves successful at something [. . .]'

It was argued that, with appropriate support, these pupils could be integrated into the mainstream and given opportunities to redeem themselves and gain success through the formal curriculum, and that success would be more likely in the redesigned curriculum.

The first step in the integration process was to relocate the MLD unit in the main buildings of the school (previously it had occupied a group of demountable classrooms in the playground). From then on, through careful monitoring of staff opinion, the programme gained pace. Initially, a few volunteers from among the mainstream teachers began to work alongside the SEN teachers. As this developed, arrangements began to be made for MLD pupils to take part in some mainstream classes. At no time were teachers forced to take part in this exercise. Gradually, however, the programme developed its own momentum, with more staff wishing to be involved. The programme was supported by in-service training, and eventually, after five years, the MLD unit was formally disbanded as a separate entity. Former MLD staff became the core of the Curriculum Support faculty, and all pupils were now integrated into the mainstream timetable, with support staff working alongside mainstream staff. For Ms Lincoln, the key to the success of the programme was a willingness to proceed at the pace dictated by the staff; only when there were signs of sufficient confidence and willingness would the next stage in the integration programme take place. The result is that staff now feel committed to the concept of integration, because they have made it work in their school, through their own efforts. Ms Lincoln claims that the staff development interviews show a resounding endorsement for this policy. This is further supported by a recent move, urged by staff, to disperse the MLD pupils across all teaching groups, as opposed to restricting them to one half of each year group, as senior management had proposed.

REFORMING THE PASTORAL SYSTEM

The introduction of the new curriculum and the integration of disruptive and SEN pupils into the mainstream were innovations which brought with them the need for staff to reassess their teaching approaches. Staff underwent in-service training for mixed-ability teaching and gradually began to experience a broadening of their functions as class teachers. This change led to an examination of the pastoral system in the school. Previously the pastoral system had functioned essentially as a crisis intervention service, charged mainly with the responsibility of relieving mainstream teachers of troublesome pupils. Increasingly, staff were taking responsibility in their classrooms for developing strategies for dealing with behaviour problems, and a discipline system was developed (see below) which sought curricular remedies to discipline problems as a first resort. Thus, subject departments and mainstream teachers were increasingly taking over many of the pastoral functions that had been delegated under the old system. To complement this, the pastoral staff now had their roles redesigned, so that they became much more concerned than they had been previously with their pupils' academic progress. Heads of year began to take on the role of 'curriculum co-ordinators', whose job it was to monitor the state of the curriculum in their year group. The thinking behind this change was based on the growing recognition among staff that emotional and behavioural problems often had their beginnings in problems associated with the curriculum, whether it be a learning difficulty or some kind of clash with a teacher.

The discipline code

The discipline code was introduced, following the consultation procedures already described, in response to staff concern that there was a lack of consistency in behavioural standards enforced by staff. The code is described by Ms Lincoln as being inspired by the Elton Report (DES, 1989a), stressing the importance of collaboration and the need for the pupils' perspective to be considered. The code is printed, in a concise form, on a single page of the staff handbook. The code divides discipline problems into three levels: Minor, Persistent and Urgent problems. Responses are divided into three stages. Stage one involves the class teacher attempting to implement a remedy through such means as 'gentle exhortations or firm reminders' and constructive punishment. The second stage involves consultation within the department, usually with the head of department. At this stage consideration might be given to the appropriateness of teaching methods, or the possibility that the pupil is placed in an unsuitable teaching group. The final stage requires the formal involvement of the pupil's form tutor, who can initiate a wide range of monitoring and intervention exercises, from monitoring the pupil's behaviour across the curriculum, to inviting parents or outside agencies, such as the Educational Psychologist, to become involved. The emphasis is clearly on adopting a low-key approach to problems so as not to cause undue escalation of a situation. Staff are encouraged to seek solutions within the classroom situation before requesting outside help. This means that staff tend to ask questions about appropriateness of learning experiences that are being offered to pupils, and so not simply jump to the conclusion that pupils are always to blame for their failure to conform to expectations. This applies at the department level also: higher levels of intervention (i.e. stages two and three) are only invoked once lower levels have been shown to be ineffective. Although this system appears to place a greater responsibility on the shoulders of class teachers than they experienced previously, when misbehaviour was almost always dealt with by the head of year, the staff are also aware of a formal support network of colleagues to whom a situation can be referred when their own attempted solutions fail. In addition to these measures there is also a system for dealing with 'urgent and major problems' which require immediate classroom support. This is dealt with by the provision of a rota of senior staff who are required to provide the necessary personal support at a given time.

The reward system

In keeping with the move away from coercive styles of pupil management, and a growing emphasis on the need to provide pupils with positive opportunities for formal success and recognition, a reward system was introduced by staff. Once again the Elton Report was used as a source by staff at one of their workshops. A major concern voiced by staff was the lack of rewards being made available for pupils in the middle- and lower-ability ranges. It was felt by staff that the general level of pupil motivation and commitment to the school would be raised if rewards and recognition were extended to all pupils, and not just the academically successful. On the basis of this staff were consulted as to the range of criteria that they felt to be appropriate for formal rewards. The following list was produced:

- academic excellence – either outstanding pieces of work, or consistent achievement at a high standard;
- diligence/effort – might be shown by improvement in any area;
- service to others;
- sport;
- extra-curricular activities.

On the basis of staff comments, which are made in writing and passed on to tutors, pupils can earn Certificates of Commendation, which are formally awarded at full school assemblies. In addition, pupils can receive 'exceptional praise' from within a particular subject area or department, and are accordingly presented with an award by the appropriate head of department or faculty.

Along with the reward system, a school council has also been instituted at the school. The council has representatives from each tutor group and, as well as offering pupils a voice which is heard by the school management, it also has a small budget at its disposal which it administers in accordance with its members' concerns.

The counselling programme

The appointment of a half-time professional school counsellor was made in response to staff concern about their lack of expertise in dealing with many of the emotional problems which they believed to be at the root of some of the more severe and intractable emotional and behavioural problems that were evident among pupils. As John Williams, a deputy head, put it:

> We saw it [the appointment of a counsellor] as a way of coming to terms with some of the issues that we were, like many other schools, having to cope with children who can't have social relationships; children who are out of their depth, perhaps in sexual relationships or emotional problems at home such as family break up, serious family illness or bereavement, peer group relationships, financial difficulties at home. These are the sorts of major issues that run through [relationships in school]. These things come out in confrontations with staff, feeling that they [pupils] can't cope; that everything's just too much.

The staff response to this situation exemplifies the confident and constructive approach to problem solving that this staff group has undertaken under the leadership of Ms Lincoln.

The counselling programme operates as a service for pupils, and is, in many ways, quite separate from the formal organisation of the school. Pupils can be referred to the counsellor by staff or they can be self-referring. Even when referred by staff, however, their involvement in counselling is strictly voluntary. Pupils refer themselves by making an appointment with the counsellor, and counselling sessions take place during school time. When self-referring, the counsellor merely provides the name of the pupil to senior management; the details of counselling sessions are protected by a code of absolute confidentiality. The counsellor operates a 'person-centred' approach (Rogers, 1951), which is non-directive and aims to mobilise clients' own inner resources to come to terms and combat their difficulties. The programme has been successful, and the number of self-referrals has increased considerably in the three years since it was introduced. In the year 1989–90 13 per cent of pupils at the Valley attended formal counselling sessions (i.e. a programme of at least six one-hour sessions). In addition, a much larger group of pupils has had informal contact with the counsellor, during breaks and lunchtimes. Referrals cover a wide range of problems including: academic difficulties, family difficulties, peer group and interpersonal conflict, behaviour problems in and out of school; personal problems relating to self-image are also common. Other problems include: sexual abuse, substance abuse and pregnancy.

The counselling programme epitomises the shift away from coercive approaches to pupil non-conformity and a move towards a recognition of the complex and individual needs of the pupils at the Valley School. As such it is fully consistent with the other reforms outlined here.

MANAGEMENT AND STAFF

The quality of leadership is an enduring feature of effective schools, and the Valley School is no exception. As has already been shown, Ms Lincoln combines an open and consultative style of management with a certain forthrightness. The evidence of staff development interviews and the reports of workshops indicate that her staff share with her a common set of values, in their efforts to improve the school. This state of affairs was not, however, achieved overnight. Ms Lincoln estimates that there has been between 30 and 40 per cent turnover among staff since she took over, among these the majority of heads of department in the core subjects. On the positive side there have been a number of internal promotions, and new staff brought in over the last few years have tended to stay. Ms Lincoln believes that the school offers staff the opportunity to 'find a niche here' because their strengths and enthusiasms will be valued and encouraged to develop. The changes in the staff group have also enabled her and her management team to select new staff who appear already sympathetic to the kind of school they are trying to build. Ms Lincoln describes the qualities she looks for in staff in the following terms:

> I won't appoint anybody who doesn't believe in comprehensive education. The most important thing for me is that they believe in comprehensive education. I don't need enemies amongst my staff. Every member of my staff is an image maker. They've got to go out there, and whatever they do – even if they're buying at the market on a Saturday – they're selling the school. And if they're

in Tesco's supermarket in a queue, and somebody says to them, 'How's that ropey place of yours [the Valley School] these days?' I want them to reply, saying, 'It's a good place that, and I'm proud to work there.' [. . .] If they don't believe what I believe in about what comprehensive education is about, then please look elsewhere!

The next thing I look for is relationships: how are they with children? Do they categorise children? Do they stigmatise children? Or, do they see every child as somebody's loved one to be developed, and made into what the school will be proud of, and the parents proud of too?

And I think, thirdly, would be the academic breadth of what they can teach. I mean, under LMS [Local Management of Schools], I can't afford to take anybody who can't teach up to 'A' Level in a subject, because of this being a 13 to 18 school.

In these three qualities we see a reflection of the major achievement of the school, in terms of the school's move towards offering a truly comprehensive education to all its pupils, and its determination to create a caring and supportive community to which staff and pupils are proud to belong. On this latter point, a significant change is that now, of all the heads of department and faculty in the school with secondary age children of their own, only one does not send his own children to the Valley School, as compared with there being no staff with children at the school when Mrs Lincoln took over in 1984.

OUTCOMES

An important aspect of the innovation programme at the Valley has been regular evaluation reports. Where appropriate these collate statistical evidence as well as (and sometimes more importantly) staff views. Key outcomes to date are seen to be:

- improved GCSE results (from 10 per cent achieving 'C' grade or better in 1985/6 to 28 per cent in 1990);
- truancy rates down sharply;
- improved staff satisfaction with classroom discipline;

- improved staff satisfaction with the quality of staff–pupil relationships;
- reduced levels of vandalism and graffiti in school;
- reduced numbers of pupils being excluded and expelled;
- dramatically reduced number of pupils being brought before the courts for offending;
- increased numbers of pupils from outside the catchment area seeking places at the school;
- improved staying on rates, contributing to a 6.7 per cent increase in the size of the 6th form (leading to recalculation of school's LMS budget).

Interviews with a small group of pupils identified by staff as having difficulties adjusting to the school bear out many of the points made above. Many of these pupils refer to the supportive efforts of staff and the school counsellor in particular as being instrumental in saving their school careers, for example:

When I first joined the school I had quite a bad temper. But, after a while, it all calmed down a bit, with the help of Janet, the counsellor. [. . .] I definitely wouldn't still be here without the help of Janet. I'd probably be at another school, or at home with a home tutor, or something. With the help I've had from the school counsellor, it gave me an insight into my inner temperament. And I've calmed myself down a bit.

(year 11 boy)

Mr Fordyce is really good, he's a caring kind of teacher, and he's helped me out with any situation, if he's got the time. He'll usually make time. You can see him any time, unless he's teaching, and then you just catch up with him at breaktime.

(year 11 boy)

With a counsellor, if you need somebody to talk to – say you're really depressed and messy – and you really need somebody to talk to, you can come to her and arrange an appointment. Cos otherwise, like me, I bottle it all up. And if the teacher had a go at me or anything, like I've done before, I've ended up walking out; having a right go at the teacher, which I know is wrong. [. . .] Before the counsellor

170

came, I was forever shouting at teachers and walking out of lessons, and screaming at them. I even went to hit one once: Mr Smythe – I never got on with Mr Smythe, ever. [. . .] And then I started seeing the counsellor, and my relationship with Mr Smythe changed completely. [. . .] I think it was me changed Mr Smythe, because I changed my attitude towards him.

(year 12 girl)

Some of the staff here have got a lot of time for the pupils. I mean a lot of them bend over backwards to keep you here. Like when I was in all my trouble in the first year [. . .] I wouldn't want to go to any other school. Cos I mean, when I got kicked out last time, I got the choice to go to [three other schools]. None of them were good enough really. My parents say this is the best school in the county, and I agree with them.

(year 11 boy)

These pupils encapsulate a significant part of the Valley School's achievement in their description of a school setting which provides mechanisms which have proved effective in helping them to solve difficulties which might have led to their being deprived of educational opportunities. For these pupils, the school counsellor, in particular, provides them with respite from in-school difficulties, which may or may not relate to out-of-school difficulties, and opportunities to come to terms with their own behaviour.

On the wider front we have seen how the staff of the Valley School have worked to create a school institution which attempts to offer all its pupils opportunities for success in a variety of ways, against a background of supportive staff–pupil relationships, and opportunities within the system to obtain respite from circumstances which might threaten their chances of taking advantage of the educational opportunities, and help in overcoming difficulties.

CONCLUSION

In the last two chapters we have explored the practicalities of school effectiveness with particular reference to emotional and behavioural difficulties. A particular feature of these chapters has been the consideration of one group of pupils' perspectivesoneffectiveness,andthecircumstancestheybelieve to be conducive to the effective educational treatment of emotional and behavioural problems. We can conclude that the concepts of respite, relationships and opportunities (re-signification), which were central to the pupils' accounts of their experience of effective schooling, can be seen to fit well with the activities reported as taking place at the Valley School. One hypothesis that might emerge from this account is:

> Schools where pupils experience conditions characterised by opportunities for respite from in-school and out-of-school difficulties, good quality relationships with staff and opportunities to achieve rewards and recognition in a wide range of areas (including academic, personal and social development), are likely to experience lower rates of emotional and behavioural problems than schools of similar social make up where the pupils experience deficiencies in these areas.

A key point to be noted here is the importance that is attached to seeing emotional and behavioural problems within a whole school context, and recognising that all aspects of the school community impinge in different ways on pupils' personal states and sense of well-being. The study of the Valley School shows how these three conditions have been brought about in a failing mainstream school, through the use of management techniques which, the next chapter will show, reflect those identified by school effectiveness researchers, in their emphasis on strong leadership, consultation and effective communication.

9

TOWARDS SCHOOL
EFFECTIVENESS

The last two chapters have explored the concept of school effectiveness through reference to the quality of both special and ordinary school provision. This exploration was developed by examining the perceptions of the key participants in school life (pupils and staff) and by considering a case study illustrating some of the processes of institutional change involved in enhancing effectiveness. In this chapter, we look in more detail at the notion of the effective school and examine how any school, as an institution, can apply theory to practice in developing strategies for dealing with pupils who present emotional and behaviour difficulties.

In recent years, school effectiveness research has had an increasingly pervasive influence on schooling. International interest in the area is demonstrated by the growing list of publications which advocate approaches to school management and organisation which are informed by insights gained from this research (see, for example, Purkey and Smith, 1983 (USA); Beare *et al.*, 1989 (Australia); and Mortimore *et al.*, 1988 (England)). In this chapter, consideration is given to some of the practical implications which school effectiveness research has for the occurrence of emotional and behavioural difficulties in mainstream and special schools. The argument of this chapter is that the institutional arrangements in schools have a profound influence on the social and emotional adjustment of their students and that schools have it in their power to inhibit, or exacerbate, the development of emotional and behavioural difficulties and to function as effective therapeutic agents.

SCHOOL EFFECTIVENESS STUDIES

Key British school effectiveness studies include: the study of twelve Inner London comprehensive schools (Rutter *et al.*, 1979); the study of eight comprehensive schools in South Wales (Reynolds, 1976, 1984; Reynolds and Sullivan, 1979, 1981); the study of 50 junior schools (Mortimore *et al.*, 1988); and the study of 20 urban comprehensive schools (Smith and Tomlinson, 1989). Although these studies each employed different approaches, they all found statistically significant differences between the schools they studied, in terms of levels of pupil achievement (as measured by examination pass rates, scores on standardised tests of reading and verbal reasoning), pupil attendance and pupil behaviour (as measured by standardised assessment procedures, teacher perceptions and observation), which could not be explained in terms of intake variables, such as pupils' measured ability levels, or the socio-economic status of pupils' families and other social and individual factors. Levels of resourcing and the quality of school buildings also appeared to bear no relation to these outcomes. Behaviour, attendance and achievement, however, did appear to be related, in the sense that where schools performed well on one of these variables, they tended to perform well on the other two; the converse was also true. The common conclusion to be drawn from these studies, therefore, is that factors within the schools themselves were responsible for the variations in pupil outcomes.

Although some of the earlier studies among these have been criticised on methodological grounds, their main contentions have received wide acceptance, and given impetus to advocates of school improvement by underlining the important role of the school in influencing pupil outcomes (Purkey and Smith, 1983; Reid *et al.*, 1987). This is exemplified in reports by HMI (1977, 1979, 1985), and the recent Elton Report (DES, 1989a) which cites school effectiveness research as one of the underpinnings for its recommendations relating to whole school approaches to pupil discipline.

School effectiveness research, however, does not undermine the long-held view that socio-economic factors have a powerful influence on the educational outcomes achieved by pupils. It is still the case that pupils from socially disadvantaged and marginalised social groups tend to perform less well and achieve relatively lower educational outcomes than their more advantaged peers; this is so even in so-called 'effective schools' (Mortimore *et al.*, 1988). What the school effectiveness researchers show is that individual schools can have the effect of magnifying or reducing the impact of negative social influences on pupil outcomes; they cannot remove these influences altogether. It is not the case that the most effective schools are those where most pupils achieve high academic outcomes, where attendance is the highest in comparison with other schools, and where there is the lowest incidence of behaviour problems. The most effective schools are those which have better outcomes in comparison to schools serving similar pupil intakes. This point is absolutely fundamental to an understanding of school effectiveness.

SCHOOL EFFECTIVENESS AND EMOTIONAL AND BEHAVIOURAL DIFFICULTIES

Charlton and David (1990) provide a comprehensive summary of the key characteristics of effective schools which have been identified by school effectiveness researchers as being associated with the low incidence of behaviour problems. While many of these points have emerged from the study of ordinary schools they would appear to be equally relevant to special schools and units. The factors to which they refer are:

1　methods of leadership by senior management which involve consultation with colleagues and take account of the opinions of parents and pupils;
2　a common school-wide policy which establishes clear academic and behavioural expectations that are realistic and meaningful to pupils, and which are consistently and humanely enforced;
3　a curriculum which is matched to pupils' present and future needs;
4　high, but not unreasonable, academic expectations;
5　a positive approach to pupil behaviour, which emphasises the use of rewards for good behaviour rather than the imposition of punishments for bad behaviour;

6 care and vigilance by staff in efficient planning and setting, and prompt marking of pupil work; adherence to starting and ending times of lessons;

7 teachers who employ skills to arouse pupil interest and motivate them to work well;

8 approaches to classroom management which emphasise the anticipation and prevention of behaviour problems, rather than reacting to them when they arise;

9 supportive and respectful relationships amongst teachers, between teachers and pupils, amongst pupils, between the school and parents, and between the school and outside agencies;

10 opportunities for pupils to become involved in, and share responsibility for, the running of the school;

11 an effective system of pastoral care.

While the experienced teacher may find many items in this list compatible with their commonsense understandings of what makes a good school, the precise ways in which these factors function to influence the behaviour and motivation of pupils are not wholly understood. It is important, for instance, to recognise that the same teacher actions performed in two different schools, with apparently similar pupil intakes, sometimes produce entirely different pupil behaviours, so that a teacher's leaving a class unsupervised during a lesson in school A produces mayhem, whilst in school B the pupils continue to work diligently (Rutter *et al.*, 1979). This suggests that this same act is assigned a different meaning in each of these schools, and different meanings often invoke different responses. This is where the concept of 'ethos' comes in.

'Ethos' describes the values and attitudes that underpin the social organisation of the school. Ethos is experienced as the overall tone, social climate and atmosphere of a school. It is exemplified in the quality of interaction between teachers and pupils, teachers' approaches to pupil management and the degree of care and attention that is given to the maintenance and appearance of buildings and classrooms. Of central importance here are the social and physical conditions that are experienced by pupils.

Positive school ethos has been described by researchers as being associated with co-operative relationships and purposeful joint planning activities among staff, a shared commitment among staff and pupils to positive educational and institutional values and goals (Reid *et al.*, 1987). The implication is that pupils in effective schools have a powerful sense of their own self-worth and potential for achievement, which is fostered by positive staff attitudes and behaviour; descriptors which are strikingly similar to those advocated by Wills (1960) in relation to the therapeutic environment needed in a special school and referred to in Chapter 3.

Reynolds and Sullivan (1979, 1981), in their study of eight comprehensive schools in South Wales, found the more effective schools to be characterised by an ethos of 'incorporation', whilst the least effective schools displayed an ethos of 'coercion'. These modes of social organisation and patterns of interaction were seen to reflect the differences in ethos. The staff in the coercive schools held negative attitudes towards their pupils, seeing them as being in need of containment, control and character training. They employed deficiency and deprivation explanations for the high levels of learning and behavioural difficulty they observed in their pupils. Teaching and management strategies that were associated with this view tended towards the punitive and confrontational; staff–pupil relationships were, by and large, of an impersonal nature. The incorporative ethos, however, was characterised by the teachers' positive view of pupils and their parents, a recognition of the essential worth and individuality of each child, and a commitment to the aim of eliciting the voluntary involvement of pupils and their parents in school life. Teaching and management strategies associated with the incorporative ethos stressed pupil responsibility, self-discipline and involvement, both in lessons and in the wider life of the school. Staff–pupil relationships tended to be marked by an interpersonal rather than impersonal style, with the stress being on mutual respect and partnership. Learning and behaviour problems tended to be approached in a therapeutic manner, with the emphasis being on the pupils' need for support.

In many ways, of course, although Reynolds and Sullivan tend to see the patterns of school organisation as being determined by staff attitudes, it is probably more accurate to think of the relationship between attitudes and organisation as interactional rather than unidirectional. It is reasonable to hypothesise, on the basis of research into teacher and pupil perspectives on classroom disruption, that staff in 'coercive' schools see the behaviour and attainments of their pupils as justification for their negative attitudes (Hargreaves *et al.*, 1975), and disruptive pupils in such schools often feel their negative behaviour to be a justifiable response to coercive treatment (Rosser and Harré, 1976; Tattum, 1982); whilst in the 'incorporative' schools a similarly self-fulfilling prophecy may be at work. Furthermore, the prevailing ethos in a school can have a powerful influence on the attitudes and behaviours of new members of the school community. Beginning teachers tend to develop patterns of working which meet with the approval of their more established colleagues, even when these styles of working conflict with their original attitudes and educational values; as a result their attitudes begin to change to be in line with their work practices (Denscombe, 1985). Pupils are also subject to the influence of the prevailing culture of the school, adopting modes of adaptation to the institution which serve to perpetuate the prevailing culture, whether they benefit the pupils or not (Schostak, 1983).

When considered at a high level of generality the characteristics of effective schools are fairly unproblematic. If we look back to the key characteristics, listed above, we find three (1, 2 and 7) of the characteristics making direct reference to the pupils' perceptions of organisational, disciplinary and academic areas of school life. These factors, in addition to those referring to the importance of placing pupil needs in the forefront of curriculum design (item 3), high academic expectation (item 4), the emphasis on rewards for good behaviour and work (item 5), mutually rewarding staff–pupil relationships (item 9), pupil participation in the running of the school (item 10), and an effective pastoral system (11), all suggest a commitment to the pupil as an active and valued participant in school life, and imply an image of the pupil as one of a group of worthy individuals, in need of care, consideration and nurture. Items also refer to the importance of collaborative and co-operative relationships within the staff group, which indicate effective leadership, a clear sense of direction and a consensus of values and purpose (1, 2 and 9).

When we consider the range of practical measures that effective schools employ to achieve these outcomes, however, things begin to look a little less straightforward. For example, whilst Reynolds and Sullivan associated the use of therapeutic, as opposed to punitive, responses to pupil misbehaviour with school effectiveness, Rutter *et al.* (1979) found that the most effective schools in their study tended to employ a 'disciplinary', rather than therapeutic, approach to similar problems. Similarly, Rutter *et al.* suggest that tightly structured school organisations, which exert a high degree of institutional control over pupils, tend to be more effective, whilst Reynolds and Sullivan find such characteristics associated with ineffective schools. A further example is provided by Galloway (1985a) who, in considering the merits of different pastoral care systems, argues that no system can claim to be more effective than another, in terms of the quality of the pastoral care provided to pupils, *per se*. He posits that pastoral effectiveness depends upon the commitments and orientations of the staff who implement the system.

In relation to the therapeutic versus disciplinary debate, it is important to note that effective schools adopting a disciplinary approach tended to employ the approach with less frequency than their less effective counterparts. This suggests that the appropriate point of comparison between the schools from the two studies is not the response systems, in relation to behaviour problems, but the broader principles underpinning the different schools' approach to behavioural problems.

A strong feature of the effective schools reported by Rutter *et al.* was the use of preventive rather than reactive measures. By implication, it would seem to be the case that, in these effective schools, the preventive programme was so successful that the disciplinary response was a far less significant aspect of school life than it was in the comparatively less effective schools. It follows, as with the pastoral care issue, that any meaningful description of the way in which a given institutional feature actually functions within an institution must be conceived in terms of the way in which that feature is understood and experienced by the people who operate within the institution. If, therefore, we are to attempt to unravel the mechanisms which produce effectiveness, it is necessary to uncover the everyday understandings and perceptions of staff and pupils in particular schools.

The value of this approach is exemplified in an action research project described by Badger (1992). In this study a range of quantitative and qualitative data is gathered on the incidence of, and perceptions surrounding, disruptive behaviour in a school. An action plan is then devised by the staff, in order to deal with problems identified in the research. Key areas of concern to emerge are:

1 organisational factors (such as grouping of pupils, length of lessons, timetabling);
2 matters of ethos (such as consistency of rules observed by staff, the need for positive sanctions);
3 teacher behaviour (including their ways of relating to pupils, punctuality in lessons).

To summarise: given the complexities of school organisation and the puzzling differences that exist between outwardly similar schools, it is extremely unwise to presume that what works in one school will necessarily work in another. However, if we take the conclusions of school effectiveness researchers and consider them in relation to the studies presented in Chapters 7 and 8 of the present book, we can suggest with some confidence that what effective schools seem to share in common, is a high level of internal consistency of approach among staff, which leads to forms of organisation and interaction that work for the benefit of pupils' social, personal and academic development. It is the school experience which is critical here: the ways in which staff and pupils interpret and make sense of their circumstances and thus socially construct their institutions.

THE PROCESS OF INSTITUTIONAL CHANGE

Perhaps because school responses to problem behaviour have often not given sufficient attention to the theoretical rationale which underpins them or have espoused one approach to the exclusion of all others, changing behaviour policy in institutions has often been a slow and haphazard process. One considerable benefit of recent educational reforms ought to be a more consistent and less piecemeal system for school development. This will apply to special as well as ordinary schools, though it may be particularly beneficial for pupils with emotional and behaviour difficulties in the latter.

Ever since the Warnock Report (DES, 1978) and the 1981 Education Act, there has been an increased emphasis on the merits of maintaining children with special needs in mainstream settings, wherever possible. This has been partly in response to concerns about 'labelling' or stigmatising groups of pupils through segregation and also because of the lack of research evidence to demonstrate that separate provision does actually produce identifiable benefits for the pupils to whom it is offered (Galloway and Goodwin, 1987). Although it can be argued that recent educational reforms may in fact be reversing the trend towards integration, as schools seek the removal of pupils who are seen as too demanding of time and limited resources (Smith, 1992b), support within the mainstream could be enhanced, if provision for pupils with emotional and behavioural difficulties is accepted as a central part of school development plans rather than a peripheral concern for a few specialist teachers.

The focus on institutional change necessary to accommodate new arrangements for the curriculum and management of schools could provide the stimulus and impetus for a fresh appraisal of policies in this area. In particular, it is proposed in the 1993 Education Bill that schools will be required to report annually on their policies for meeting special educational needs, including information about teaching strategies, such as staffing, withdrawal and support (Peter, 1993). Though existing school annual reports are usually bland to the point of opacity, this formal requirement will enable interested teachers, governors and parents to use this administrative lever to prise open the barriers of indifference to special needs still encountered in many mainstream schools.

An appropriate structure for consultation, planning and organisation already exists, which can readily be adapted to focus particularly on the needs of pupils with emotional and behavioural difficulties. Smith (1991) suggests that the National Curriculum Council (NCC, 1989) advice on the four elements which should be considered in planning the curriculum for pupils with special educational needs in ordinary schools, offers a structure which can be adapted to analyse how successfully institutions are working with pupils with emotional and behavioural difficulties. These four elements are:

- a development plan;
- schemes of work;
- learning environment;
- individual teaching needs.

A development plan

Whether in ordinary or special school or unit, preparing and approving a school development plan begins with the collection and collation of information about what is actually happening within the school, as Stone (1990) puts it: 'where the school is now, what is working well, what areas need attention and how this attention is to be given'.

In terms of monitoring the effectiveness of educational responses to problem behaviour, this gathering of information would be the starting point for a close scrutiny of whether the school is achieving its aims, whether teaching methods and styles are suited to its intended philosophical stance or psychological approach. For special schools, this would be the occasion to review whether they do see themselves as engaged in dynamic psychotherapy or behaviour modification or, if a bit of both, whether the two are really compatible. Is the special school or unit 'milieu' geared to offering respite, encouraging relationships and promoting re-signification as suggested in Chapter 7, and if so, how? Are mainstream school policies on discipline and pastoral care in need of reappraisal as happened in the Valley School as reported in Chapter 8?

This process of scrutiny should involve a critical look at human and physical resources and at how these are being deployed. This is the stage at which the school examines and debates its theory, its rationale and its purpose. This can then lead to a written statement of aims and objectives or, in the language of business management, which nowadays increasingly encroaches on the world of education, its 'mission statement'. At this level the institution will be identifying its priorities and targets for organisational change. At each of the other stages, institutional change will involve identifying and answering specific questions about how effectively these targets are being attained in practice. This first stage is the point at which reflection on the issues raised in the introduction and Part I of this book will help participants identify their philosophical and methodological stance and question whether other views may have something to offer.

Schemes of work

At the next stage, the focus is on what has been described in Chapter 6 as 'monitoring', investigating the effectiveness of school organisation and management in realising intended objectives. At this point, familiarity with the examples of institutional change in Chapters 7 and 8 will help draw attention to the factors involved in developing and implementing whole school policies which take account of pupil and staff perspectives.

In schools and units for pupils with emotional and behavioural difficulties, the audit of schemes of work, which the NCC document refers to as written definitions of work to be done in subject areas over a specific period of time, could be accompanied by a similar 'audit of care', which examines and sets out in writing responsibilities of members of care and teaching staff, particularly in dealing with serious incidents and emergencies. This should also be the stage at which all schools consider policies on rewards, sanctions, counselling and guidance, picking up, for example, on whether these are consistent with an institution's perceived role in offering a particular kind of milieu or psychotherapy. What is the school's rationale for its policies on behaviour and discipline and do all members of staff feel a sense of ownership of them? Do pupils understand and accept the reasoning behind the way in which they are treated? For special schools, this may also be the point at which to assess what exactly is the difference in their curriculum or regime, which gives substance to the claim that what they offer could not be provided in the mainstream.

Learning environment

At the next stage, consideration of the learning environment will focus attention more directly on how institutional policy is translated into practice through interaction between staff and pupils. Here knowledge of the different approaches outlined in Part II of this book will help analyse the techniques through which teachers attempt to mediate or modify behaviour. Tattum (1986) outlines the concept of 'consistency management' to describe the process whereby schools monitor whether teachers' planning, preparation and practice puts enunciated policy into actual operation. This should raise questions about what are the rules which set boundaries for acceptable behaviour and what are the routines which regulate the flow of activities within classrooms. Are staff agreed on what school rules should be and do pupils have some say in how they are formulated? This is the stage at which to check records and evaluate progress, to see whether modification programmes are working or not, to examine whether reward systems are providing reinforcement and whether sanctions are being consistently applied. If less directive approaches are the chosen style, these can also be evaluated in terms of personal progress for pupils and organisational support for staff. If the ecosystemic approach is favoured, what changes have been made and what has been their effect?

Individual teaching needs

Finally, the concept of individual teaching needs also implies individual management needs, especially for pupils whose difficulties in forming and maintaining relationships make confrontation a frequent possibility and additional support a certain necessity. What arrangements are made to see that teachers are sensitive to the importance of differentiation of learning materials and behavioural expectations for individual pupils? What guidance is given on how teachers should manage difficulties if they do arise? Here the chapters from Part II are again relevant, with the focus of attention shifted more towards the individual teacher's personal responsibility for management in the classroom but there is also still an institutional responsibility for making sure that there is appropriate guidance and support. What arrangements are made for in-service training and professional development to ensure that all teachers are aware of recent developments in thinking and practice in work with pupils with emotional and behavioural difficulties? What opportunities exist for observing and learning from colleagues within the school or elsewhere, about successful application of psychodynamic, behavioural or ecosystemic techniques?

APPRAISE, ANALYSE AND ADAPT

Systematic scrutiny of the above four aspects of school organisation and management will ensure that long-term strategies are kept under review, but schools also have to develop procedures for more immediate short-term crisis intervention. Once again, opportunities to apply theory to practice will be enhanced by a systematic approach, through which an action plan can be formulated. The following model involves three stages in which teachers are encouraged to appraise, analyse and adapt their responses to emotional and behaviour difficulties.

Appraise

Define the problem in terms of:

- Who recognises the problem?
- Who is involved in its solution?
- How do the different people involved construe the problem situation?

Consider:

1 the classroom situation: teacher–pupil interaction (interpersonal and social), pupil–pupil interaction (interpersonal and social), pattern of organisation;
2 the wider institutional context: school ethos, links between in-class behaviour and out-of-class factors, relationships among staff;

3 out-of-school factors: affecting pupil and/or teacher behaviour and emotional states (e.g. family or peer group influences).

Analyse

Look for possible solutions:

1 at the immediate classroom level: what can the classroom teacher do to alleviate the problem? (appropriateness of teaching methods, management or organisational change? appropriate balance of rewards and sanctions in the classroom? perceptual change? manner of relating to pupils? implications for in-service training for individual?);
2 what support can be given to the class teacher to enable him or her to deal effectively with the problem? (pastoral care team? departmental support? peer support group? use of support staff? external consultants: e.g. educational psychology, special needs advisory service?);
3 what support can be given to the pupil? (peer support? pastoral care team? counselling? external consultants?);
4 are changes in the broader school context appropriate? (time-table? curriculum? grouping of pupils? appropriate balance between rewards and sanctions within school? implications for in-service training for the staff as a whole?);
5 is the context outside the school most likely to yield a solution? (family problems, involvement of other agencies? use of external consultants?).

Adapt

Putting preferred solution into action and monitoring its effectiveness:

1 ensure that all people who might affect, or be affected by, the proposed solution (both in and out of school) are informed of what is happening and what they can do to support the endeavour;
2 set clear goals to establish whether or not the solution has worked (e.g. specify desired behavioural change);

3 set up monitoring system, specify: how solution will be monitored (observation schedule, interview, written/verbal reports); who will do the monitoring; where and when and to whom results will be reported and what is the timescale for the intervention;
4 put plan into action;
5 review, maintaining consultation;
6 return to earlier stage and appraise and analyse again, if plan is not working.

The first two stages can be carried out by individuals at all levels in the school hierarchy. Whoever is responsible, wide consultation including parents and pupils will be helpful. At the third stage, the way in which the problem is framed, the solution selected and the decision-making structures in the school will determine who is responsible for implementation. Again, consultation and sharing of information as widely as possible, provided that this does not compromise individual rights to privacy, will be very beneficial.

The chapters of this book dealing with behavioural approaches (Chapter 4), ecosystemic approaches (Chapter 5) and classroom management (Chapter 6) offer many suggestions about possible solutions at stage three, and the nature of appraisal and analysis may well reflect the school's view of the nature and development of emotional and behavioural difficulties (Chapter 1) and its role in responding to them (Chapter 2).

There are some general questions, which will help individuals in reflecting on their own teaching or support schools in the development process, whether for long- or short-term planning and organisation:

1 Does this school/class provide a supportive environment for *all* pupils, in an affective sense?
2 Are behavioural and educational expectations appropriate, sufficiently high and explicit?
3 How successfully are *all* pupils personally involved in appropriate, well-structured and clearly purposeful activities?
4 Is there a continuous focus for pupil activity and a sense of progression in learning programmes?

5 Is teaching responsive to *all* pupils giving them opportunities for success and recognition?
6 Is there a positive model of personal acceptance and respect for individual differences?
7 What is it like to be a pupil inside this school and how is the school seen by parents and others on the outside?

Considering these questions will help determine priorities for change and improvement. Chapters 7 and 8 might provide starting points for discussion because they show how these issues have been addressed in other schools. This book has been written to extend knowledge and understanding of the range of theory and practice in other schools and therapeutic communities on which teachers can draw in formulating policies for helping schools become more effective in dealing with problems presented by pupils with emotional and behavioural difficulties. We are aware that Samuel Johnson once commented that one may be 'very sincere in good principles, without having good practice' but we do believe, that in teaching, it is rarely possible to have good practice without good principles and we trust that readers will agree that this book has helped them define the 'good principles', or theory, which inform their practice.

In Chapter 6, we used the term 'affirmative teaching' to describe the elements of effective school policy discussed again in this chapter. Affirmative teaching also describes the positive and confident approach of teachers, whose experience of the craft of teaching pupils with emotional and behavioural difficulties is enhanced by knowledge of the theory, which provides the rationale for what they do. Faced with problems which may appear intractable, which may arise initially from influences beyond their control, which may appear to require resources not within their possession or services not within their gift, teachers have still to ask themselves, can something be done to improve the situation? Affirmative teachers will always answer 'yes', because they are aware of a range of alternative possibilities and they are willing to try them. This does not mean flitting frequently from one strategy to another, there are skilled judgements to be made about the length of time a particular strategy may need to be given before trying something else, but we hope that, having read this book, teachers will be encouraged to have confidence in adopting and adapting new approaches to dealing with challenging behaviour.

REFERENCES

Albee, G.W. (1968) 'Models, myths and manpower', *Mental Hygiene*, 52,168–80.

Albee, G.W. (1969) 'Emerging concepts of mental illness and models of treatment: the psychological point of view', *American Journal of Psychiatry*, 125, 870–6.

Amatea, E. (1988) 'Brief systemic interventions with school behavior problems: a case of temper tantrums', *Psychology in the Schools*, 25, 2, 174–83.

Assistant Masters and Mistresses Association (1986) *A Review of the Research into the Primary Causes of Stress Among Teachers*, London: AMMA.

Ausubel, D. (1961) 'Personality disorder is disease', *American Psychologist*, 16, 69–74.

Axline, V. (1964) *Dibs*, Harmondsworth: Penguin.

Badger, B. (1992) 'Changing a disruptive school', in Reynolds, D. (ed.) *School Effectiveness: Research, Policy and Practice*, London: Cassell.

Ball, S. (1981) *Beechside Comprehensive*, Cambridge: Cambridge University Press.

Barnes, D. (1976) *From Communication to Curriculum*, Harmondsworth: Penguin.

Bateson, G. (1972) *Steps to an Ecology of Mind*, New York: Chandler.

Bateson, G. (1979) *Mind and Nature: A Necessary Unity*, New York: Dutton.

Bateson, G., Jackson, D., Haley, J. and Weakland, J. (1956) 'Towards a theory of schizophrenia', *Behavioural Science*, 1, 251–4.

Beare, J., Caldwell, J. and Millikan, R. (1989) *Creating an Excellent School*, London: Routledge.

Berger, P. and Luckman, T. (1966) *The Social Construction of Reality*, New York: Doubleday.

Berne, E. (1964) *Games People Play: The Psychology of Human Relations*, New York: Grove Press.

Bettelheim, B. (1950) *Love is Not Enough*, Glencoe, Illinois: The Free Press.

Booth, T., Potts, P. and Swann, W. (1987) *Preventing Difficulties in Learning: Curricula for All*, Oxford: Blackwell.

191

Bridge, S. and Luke, S. (1989) *Blackstone's Guide to the Children Act 1989*, London: Blackstone.

Bridgeland, M. (1971) *Pioneer Work with Maladjusted Children*, London: Staples.

Brown, D. and Pedder, J. (1979) *Introduction to Psychotherapy*, London: Tavistock Publications.

Brown, J. (1986) 'The use of paradoxical intervention with oppositional behavior in the classroom', *Psychology in the Schools*, 21, 1, 77–81.

Brown, S. and McIntyre, D. (1993) *Making Sense of Teaching*, Milton Keynes: Open University Press.

Bruner, J.S. (1966) *Towards a Theory of Instruction*, Cambridge, Mass.: Harvard University Press.

Bull, S.L. and Solity, J.E. (1987) *Classroom Management: Principles to Practice*, London: Croom Helm.

Burland, R. (1990) 'Survival skills for the comprehensive school', in Scherer, M., Gersch, I. and Fry, L. (eds) *Meeting Disruptive Behaviour: Assessment, Intervention and Partnership*, Basingstoke: Macmillan.

Bush, L. and Hill, T. (1993) 'The right to teach, the right to learn', *British Journal of Special Education*, 20, 1, 4–7.

Calderhead, J. (ed.) (1987) *Exploring Teachers' Thinking*, London: Cassell.

Campion, J. (1985) *The Child in Context: Family Systems Theory in Educational Psychology*, London: Methuen.

Canter, L. and Canter, M. (1976) *Assertive Discipline: A Take-Charge Approach for Today's Educator*, Seal Beach, California: Canter and Associates.

Carpenter, M. (1851) *Reformatory Schools for the Children of the Perishing and Dangerous Classes and for Juvenile Offenders*, London: Cash.

Charlton, T. and David, K. (eds) (1989) *Managing Misbehaviour: Strategies for Effective Management of Behaviour in Schools*, Basingstoke: Macmillan.

Charlton, T. and David, K. (1990) 'Towards a whole school approach, helping to ensure schools are fit for the future', *Links*, 15, 3, 20–4.

Chodorow, N. (1978) *The Reproduction of Mothering*, California: University of California Press.

Clark, C. and Peterson, P. (1986) 'Teachers' thought processes', in Witrock, M. (ed.) *The Handbook of Research on Teaching* (3rd edn), New York: Macmillan.

Coleman, J. and Hendry, L. (1990) *The Nature of Adolescence*, London: Routledge.

Cooper, P. (1989) 'Respite, relationships and re-signification: a study of the effects of residential schooling on pupils with emotional and behavioural difficulties, with particular reference to the pupils' perspective', unpublished PhD thesis, University of Birmingham.

Cooper, P. (1993) *Effective Schools for Disaffected Pupils: Integration and Segregation*, London: Routledge.

Cooper, P., Smith, C.J. and Upton, G. (1990) 'The qualifications and training requirements of teachers in schools for pupils with emotional and behavioural difficulties in England and Wales', *British Journal of In-Service Education*, 16, 3, 188–95.

Cooper, P., Smith, C.J. and Upton, G. (1991) 'The qualifications and training of workers for pupils with EBD', *Maladjustment and Therapeutic Education*, 9, 2, 83–7.

Cooper, P. and Upton, G (1990a) 'An ecosystemic approach to emotional and behavioural problems in schools', *Educational Psychology*, 10, 4, 301–21.

Cooper, P. and Upton, G. (1990b) 'Turning conflict into co-operation: an ecosystemic approach to interpersonal conflict and its relevance to pastoral care', *Pastoral Care in Education*, 8, 4, 10–15.

Cooper, P. and Upton, G. (1991a) 'Putting pupils' needs first', *British Journal of Special Education*, 18, 3, 111–13.

Cooper, P. and Upton, G. (1991b) 'Controlling the urge to control: an ecosystemic approach to problem behaviour in schools', *Support for Learning*, 6, 1, 22–6.

Cooper, P. and Upton, G. (1992) 'An ecosystemic approach to classroom behaviour problems', in Wheldall, K. (ed.) *Discipline in Schools: Psychological Perspectives on the Elton Report*, London: Routledge.

Copley, B. and Forryan, B. (1987) *Therapeutic Work with Children and Young People*, London: Robert Royce.

Cronk, K. (1987) *Teacher–Pupil Conflict in Secondary Schools*, Lewes: Falmer Press.

Davies, L. (1979) 'Deadlier than the male? Girls' conformity and deviance in school', in Barton, L. and Meighan, R. (eds) *Schools, Pupils and Deviance*, Driffield: Nafferton Press.

Davies, L. (1984) *Pupil Power: Deviance and Gender in School*, London: Falmer.

Davies, L. (1987) 'Viking wives at home: sexism and deviance in school', in Booth, T. and Coulby, D. (eds) *Producing and Reducing Disaffection*, Milton Keynes: Open University Press.

Denscombe, M. (1985) *Classroom Control, A Sociological Perspective*, London: Allen and Unwin.

DES (1967) *Children and their Primary Schools*, 'The Plowden Report', London: HMSO.

DES (1975) *The Discovery of Children Requiring Special Education and the Assessment of Their Needs*, Circular 2/75, London: HMSO.

DES (1978) *Report of the Committee of Enquiry into the Education of Handicapped Children and Young People*, 'The Warnock Report', London: HMSO.

DES (1985) *Education Observed: Good Teachers*, London: HMSO.

DES (1989a) *Discipline in Schools: Report of the Committee of Enquiry chaired by Lord Elton*, 'The Elton Report', London: HMSO.

DES (1989b) *Special Schools for Pupils with Emotional and Behavioural Difficulties*, Circular 23/89, London: HMSO.

de Shazer, S. (1982) *Patterns of Brief Family Therapy: An Ecosystemic Approach*, New York: Guilford.

de Shazer, S. (1985) *Keys to Solution*, New York: Norton.

Desforges, C. and McNamara, D. (1979) 'Theory and practice: methodological procedures for the objectification of craft knowledge', *British Journal of Teacher Education*, 5, 2, 145–52.

Dessent, T. (1987) *Making Ordinary Schools Special*, London: Falmer.

Dockar-Drysdale, B. (1974) *Therapy in Child Care*, London: Longman.

Dowling, E. and Osborne, E. (eds) (1985) *The Family and the School*, London: Routledge and Kegan Paul.

Dowling, E. and Taylor, D. (1989) 'The clinic goes to school: lessons learnt', *Maladjustment and Therapeutic Education*, 7, 1, 24–9.

Dreikurs, R. (1968) *Psychology in the Classroom: A Manual for Teachers*, 2nd edn, New York: Harper and Row.

Dunlop, A. (1974) *The Approved School Experience*, London: HMSO.

Dupont, H. (1969) *Educating Emotionally Disturbed Children*, New York: Holt, Rinehart and Winston.

Ellenberger, H.F. (1970) *The Discovery of the Unconscious*, London: Allen Lane.

Ellis, A. (1967) 'Should some people be labelled mentally ill?' *Journal of Consulting Psychology*, 31, 435–46.

Erikson, E.H. (1965) *Childhood and Society*, Harmondsworth: Penguin.

Evans, M. (1981) *Disruptive Pupils*, London: Schools Council.

Fletcher, C., Caron, M. and Williams, W. (1985) *Schools on Trial*, Milton Keynes: Open University Press.

Frude, N. (1984) 'Frameworks for analysis', in Frude, N. and Gault, H. *Disruptive Behaviour in Schools*, Chichester: Wiley.

Galloway, D. (1985a) 'Pastoral care and school effectiveness', in Reynolds, D. (ed.) *Studying School Effectiveness*, London: Falmer.

Galloway, D. (1985b) *Schools, Pupils and Special Educational Needs*, London: Croom Helm.

Galloway, D. and Goodwin, C. (1979) *The Education of Slow Learning and Maladjusted Children*, London: Longman.

Galloway, D. and Goodwin, C. (1987) *The Education of Disturbing Children*, Harlow: Longman.

Glasser, W. (1969) *Schools Without Failure*, New York: Harper and Row.

Glasser, W. (1975) *Reality Therapy: A New Approach to Psychiatry*, New York: Harper and Row.

Gobell, A. (1980) 'Three classroom procedures', in Upton, G. and Gobell, A. (eds) *Behaviour Problems in the Comprehensive School*, Cardiff: Faculty of Education, University College, Cardiff.

Gordon, T. (1974) *TET: Teacher Effectiveness Training*, New York: David McKay.

Graham, P. and Rutter, M. (1970) 'Identification of children with psychiatric disorder', in Rutter, M., Tizard, J. and Whitmore, K. (eds) *Education, Health and Behaviour*, London: Longman.

Gray, J. and Richer, J. (1988) *Classroom Responses to Disruptive Behaviour*, Basingstoke: Macmillan.

Gray, J. and Sime, S. (1989) 'Teachers and discipline: a report for the committee of enquiry into discipline in schools by Sheffield University', Appendix D in DES, *Discipline in Schools*, London: HMSO.

Guerin, P. and Katz, A. (1984) 'The theory in therapy of families with school related problems: triangles and a hypothesis testing model', in Okun, B. (ed.) *Family Therapy with School Related Problems*, Rockville: Aspen.

Guntrip, H. (1971) *Psycho-analytic Theory, Therapy and the Self*, London: Maresfield Reprints.

Gurney, P. (1990) 'Using behavioural contracts in the classroom', in Scherer, M., Gersch, I. and Fry, L. (eds) *Meeting Disruptive Behaviour: Assessment, Intervention and Partnership*, Basingstoke: Macmillan.

Hamblin, D. (1978) *The Teacher and Pastoral Care*, Oxford: Blackwell.

Hammersley, M. and Woods, P. (eds) (1976) *The Process of Schooling*, Milton Keynes: Open University.

Harber, C. and Meighan, R. (eds) (1989) *The Democratic School*, Ticknall: Education Now.

Hargreaves, D.H. (1967) *Social Relations in a Secondary School*, London: Routledge and Kegan Paul.

Hargreaves, D.H., Hester, S.K. and Mellor, F.J. (1975) *Deviance in Classrooms*, London: Routledge and Kegan Paul.

Harris, T.A. (1969) *I'm OK – You're OK*, New York: Harper and Row.

Hastings, J. (1981) 'One school's experience', in Gillham, B. (ed.) *Problem Behaviour in the Secondary School*, London: Croom Helm.

Herbert, M. (1978) *Conduct Disorders of Childhood and Adolescence: A Behavioural Approach to Assessment and Teaching*, Chichester: Wiley.

HMI (1977) *Ten Good Schools*, London: HMSO.

HMI (1979) *Aspects of Secondary Education*, London: HMSO.

HMI (1985) *Better Schools*, London: HMSO.

Hoffman, L. (1981) *Foundations of Family Therapy*, New York: Basic Books.

Hoghughi, M. (1978) *Troubled and Troublesome, Coping with Severely Disordered Children*, London: Burnet Books.

Hsia, H. (1984) 'Structural and strategic approaches to school phobia/school refusal', *Psychology in the Schools*, 21, 3, 360–7.

Hurlock, E.B. (1953) *Developmental Psychology*, New York: McGraw-Hill.

ILEA (1983) *Improving Secondary Schools*, London: ILEA.

ILEA (1990) *Expulsions and Exclusions from Schools*, London: ILEA.

Jones, N. (1989) 'Welfare needs in secondary schools', in Jones, N. and Southgate, T. (eds) *The Management of Special Needs in Ordinary Schools*, London: Routledge.

Jones, E. and Berrick, S. (1985) 'Adopting a resources approach', in Smith, C.J. (ed.) *New Directions in Remedial Education*, Lewes: Falmer Press.

Kanner, L. (1962) 'Emotionally disturbed children: a historical review', *Child Development*, 33, 97–102.

Keddie, N. (1971) 'Classroom knowledge', in Young, M. (ed.) *Knowledge and Control*, London: Collier-Macmillan.

Kellmer Pringle, M.L. (1974) *The Needs of Children*, London: Hutchinson.

Keys, W. and Fernandes, C. (1993) *What Do Students Think About School?* Slough: NFER.

195

REFERENCES

Kitsuse, J.I. (1962) 'Societal reactions to deviant behaviour: problems of theory and method', *Social Problems*, 9, 247–56.

Klein, M. (1932) *The Psycho-Analysis of Children*, London: Hogarth Press.

Klein, M. (1961) *Narrative of a Child Analysis*, New York: Detta.

Laslett, R. (1977) *Educating Maladjusted Children*, London: Crosby Lockwood Staples.

Laslett, R. (1983) *Changing Perceptions of Maladjusted Children 1945-1981*, London: AWMC.

Lewis, J. (1985) 'The institutional framework', in Upton, G. (ed.) *Educating Children with Behaviour Problems*, Cardiff: Faculty of Education, University College, Cardiff.

Lindquist, B., Molnar, A. and Brauchmann, L. (1987) 'Working with school related problems without going to school: considerations for systemic practice', *Journal of Strategic and Systemic Therapies*, 6, 4, 44–50.

Lloyd-Smith, M. (1984) *Disrupted Schooling: The Growth of the Special Unit*, London: John Murray.

McIntyre, D. (1991) 'The Oxford University model of teacher education', *South Pacific Journal of Teacher Education*, 19, 2, 117–29.

Macklin, R. (1972) 'Mental health and mental illness: some problems of definition and concept formation', *Philosophy of Science*, 39, 3, 341–65.

Madanes, C. (1981) *Strategic Family Therapy*, San Francisco: Jossey-Bass.

Mandel, H., Weizmann, F., Millan, B., Greenhow, J. and Speers, D. (1975) 'Reaching emotionally disturbed children: "judo" principles in remedial education', *American Journal of Orthopsychiatry*, 45, 5, 867–74.

Martin, B. (1977) *Abnormal Psychology*, New York: Holt, Rinehart and Winston.

Matza, D. (1976) 'Signification', in Hammersley, M. and Woods, P. (eds) *The Process of Schooling*, London: Routledge and Kegan Paul.

Mearns, D. and Thorne, B. (1988) *Person Centred Counselling in Action*, London: Sage.

Merrett, F. and Wheldall, K. (1986) 'Observing pupils and teachers in classrooms (OPTIC): a behavioural observation schedule for use in schools', *Educational Psychology*, 6, 57–70.

Merrick, N. and Manuel, G. (1991) 'Authorities want end to exclusion loophole', *Times Educational Supplement*, 25 October.

Miller, J. (1976) *Toward a New Psychology of Women*, London: Penguin.

Millham, S., Bullock, R. and Cherrett, R. (1975) *After Grace, Teeth, A Comparative Study of the Residential Experience of Boys in Approved Schools*, London: Chaucer.

Millham, S., Bullock, R. and Hosie, K. (1978) *Locking Up Children*, Farnborough: Saxon House.

Ministry of Education (1955) *Report of the Committee on Maladjusted Children*, 'The Underwood Report', London: HMSO.

Minuchin, S. (1974) *Families and Family Therapy*, Cambridge: Harvard University Press.

Mitchell, J. (1974) *Psychoanalysis and Feminism*, New York: Vintage.

Molnar, A. and de Shazer, S. (1987) 'Solution focused therapy: towards the identification of the therapeutic task', *Journal of Marital and Family Therapy*, 13, 4, 349–58.

Molnar, A. and Lindquist, B. (1989) *Changing Problem Behavior in Schools*, San Francisco: Jossey-Bass.

Mongon, D. (1976) 'The ambiguous problem of maladjustment', *ILEA Contact*, 5, 13, 6–7.

Mongon, D. and Hart, S. with Ace, C. and Rawlings, A. (1989) *Improving Classroom Behaviour: New Directions for Teachers and Pupils*, London: Cassell.

Morse, W. C. (1969) 'Training teachers in life space interviewing', in H. Dupont (ed.) *Educating Emotionally Disturbed Children*, New York: Holt, Rinehart and Winston.

Mortimore, P., Davies, J., Varlaam, A. and West, A. (1983) *Behaviour Problems in Schools: An Evaluation of Support Centres*, London: Croom Helm.

Mortimore, P., Sammons, L., Stoll, L. and Ecob, R. (1988) *School Matters*, London: Open Books.

National Curriculum Council (1989) *A Curriculum for All: Special Educational Needs in the National Curriculum*, Curriculum Guidance 2, London: NCC.

Neill, A.S. (1916) *A Dominie's Log*, London: Herbert Jenkins.

Neisworth, J.T. and Smith, R.M. (1973) *Modifying Retarded Behaviour*, Boston: Houghton Mifflin.

Okun, B. (1984) 'Family therapy and the schools', in Okun, B. (ed.) *Family Therapy with School Related Problems*, Rockville: Aspen.

O'Leary, K.D. and O'Leary, S.E. (1972) *Classroom Management*, New York: Pergamon.

Pavlov, I.P. (1927) *Conditioned Reflexes: An Investigation of the Physiological Activity of the Cerebral Cortex*, New York: Dover.

Peter, M. (1993) 'Amending the Education Bill', *British Journal of Special Education*, 20, 1, 3.

Power, T. and Bartholomew, K. (1985) 'Getting uncaught in the middle: a case study in family–school system consultation', *School Psychology Review*, 14, 2, 222–9.

Powney, J. and Watts, M. (1987) *Interviewing in Educational Research*, London: Routledge.

Pringle, M. (1975) *The Needs of Children*, London: Hutchinson.

Provis, M. (1992) *Dealing With Difficulty*, London: Hodder and Stoughton.

Purkey, S. and Smith, M. (1983) 'Effective schools: a review', *Elementary School Journal*, 83, 4, 427–52.

Pyke, N. (1991) 'Alarm over sharp rise in exclusions', *Times Educational Supplement*, 4 October.

Raths, L.E., Harmin, M. and Simon, S.B. (1966) *Values and Teaching*, Columbus: Merrill.

Ravenette, A.T. (1972) 'Maladjustment: clinical concept or administrative convenience?' *Journal of the Association of Educational Psychologists*, 3, 2, 41–7.

Redl, F. (1966) *When We Deal with Children*, New York: Free Press.

Redl, F. (1971) 'The concept of the life space interview', in Long, N.J., Morse, W.C. and Newman, R.G. (eds) *Conflict in the Classroom*, 2nd edn, Belmont: Wadsworth.

Redl, F. and Wineman, D. (1952) *Controls from Within*, New York: Free Press.

Reeves, C. (1983) 'Psychodynamic theory and the role of therapeutic education in a residential setting', *Maladjustment and Therapeutic Education*, 1, 2, 25–31.

Reid, K. (1985) *Truancy and School Absenteeism*, London: Hodder and Stoughton.

Reid, K., Hopkins, D. and Holly, P. (1987) *Towards the Effective School*, Oxford: Blackwell.

Reynolds, D. (1976) 'The delinquent school', in Hammersley, M. and Woods, P. (eds) *The Process of Schooling*, Milton Keynes: Open University Press.

Reynolds, D. (1984) 'The school for vandals, a sociological portrait of the disaffection prone school', in Frude, N. and Gault, H. (eds) *Disruptive Behaviour in Schools*, Chichester: Wiley.

Reynolds, D. (ed.) (1985) *Studying School Effectiveness*, London: Falmer.

Reynolds, D. and Murgatroyd, S. (1974) 'Being absent from school', *British Journal of Law and Society*, 1, 78–81.

Reynolds, D. and Reid, K. (1985) 'The second stage, towards a reconceptualisation of theory and methodology in school effectiveness research', in Reynolds, D. (ed.) *Studying School Effectiveness*, Lewes: Falmer Press.

Reynolds, D. and Sullivan, M. (1979) 'Bringing schools back in', in Barton, L. and Meighan, R. (eds) *Schools, Pupils and Deviance*, Driffield: Nafferton Books.

Reynolds, D. and Sullivan, M. (1981) 'The effects of schools, a radical faith re-stated', in Gillham, B. (ed.) *Problem Behaviour in the Secondary School*, London: Croom Helm.

Righton, P. (1975) 'Planned environmental therapy: a reappraisal', *The Journal of the Association of Workers for Maladjusted Children*, 3, 1.

Rogers, C. (1951) *Client Centred Therapy*, Boston: Houghton Mifflin.

Rogers, C. (1969) *Freedom to Learn*, Columbus: Merrill.

Rogers, C. (1980) *A Way of Being*, Boston: Houghton Mifflin.

Rogers, W.A. (1991) *'You Know the Fair Rule'*, Strategies for Making the Hard Job of Teaching Easier, Harlow: Longman.

Ross, A.O. (1968) 'Conceptual issues in the evaluation of brain damage', in Khanna, J.L. (ed.) *Brain Damage and Mental Retardation: A Psychological Evaluation*, Springfield, Illinois: Thomas.

Rosser, E. and Harré, R. (1976) 'The meaning of trouble', in Hammersley, M. and Woods, P. (eds) *The Process of Schooling*, London: Routledge and Kegan Paul.

Rutter, M. (1975) *Helping Troubled Children*, Harmondsworth: Penguin.

Rutter, M. and Giller, H. (1983) *Juvenile Delinquency, Trends and Perspectives*, Harmondsworth: Penguin.

Rutter, M., Maughan, B., Mortimore, P. and Ouston, J. (1979) *Fifteen Thousand Hours*, London: Open Books.

Scherer, M. (1990) 'Checking pupils' behavioural skills', in Scherer, M., Gersch, I. and Fry, L. (eds) *Meeting Disruptive Behaviour: Assessment, Intervention and Partnership*, Basingstoke: Macmillan.

Schostak, J. (1983) *Maladjusted Schooling*, London: Falmer.

Selvini, M. (1988) *The Work of Mara Selvini-Palazzoli*, New York: Aronson.

Selvini-Palazzoli, M., Boscolo, L., Cecchin, G. and Prata, G. (1973) *Paradox and Counterparadox*, New York: Aronson.

Sharp, R. and Green, A. (1975) *Education and Social Control*, London: Routledge and Kegan Paul.

Skinner, B.F. (1971) *Beyond Freedom and Dignity*, New York: Knopf.

Smith, A. (1978) 'Encountering the family system in school-related problems', *Psychology in the Schools*, 15, 3, 379–86.

Smith, C.J. (1977) 'Changes in provision for juvenile offenders in mid-nineteenth century England with particular reference to Merseyside', unpublished MEd dissertation, University of Liverpool.

Smith, C.J. (1990) 'The management of children with emotional and behaviour difficulties in ordinary and special schools', in Varma, V.P. (ed.) *The Management of Children with Emotional and Behavioural Difficulties*, London: Routledge.

Smith, C.J. (1991) 'Behaviour management: a whole school policy', in Hinson, M. (ed.) *Teachers and Special Educational Needs: Coping with Change*, 2nd edn, London: Longman.

Smith, C.J. (1992a) 'Keeping them clever: preventing learning difficulties from becoming behaviour problems', in Wheldall, K. (ed.) *Discipline in Schools: Psychological Perspectives on the Elton Report*, London: Routledge.

Smith, C.J. (1992b) 'Management of special needs', in Gulliford, R. and Upton, G. (eds) *Special Educational Needs*, London: Routledge.

Smith, C.J. and Laslett, R. (1993) *Effective Classroom Management: A Teacher's Guide*, 2nd edn, London: Routledge.

Smith, D. and Tomlinson, S. (1989) *The School Effect, a Study of Multi-Racial Comprehensives*, London: Policy Studies Institute.

Speed, B. (1984a) 'How really real is real?' *Family Process*, 23, 511–17.

Speed, B. (1984b) 'Family therapy: an update', *ACPCP Newsletter*, 6, 1, 2–14.

Speed, B. (1991) 'Reality exists O.K.? An argument against constructivism and social constructionism', *Journal of Family Therapy*, 13, 4, 395–409.

Stevenson, I. (1957) 'Is the human personality more plastic in infancy and childhood?' *American Journal of Psychiatry*, 114, 152–61.

Stone, L. (1990) *Managing Difficult Children in School*, Oxford: Basil Blackwell.

Swap, S., Prieto, A. and Harth, R. (1982) 'Ecological perspectives of the emotionally disturbed child', in McDowell, R., Adamson, G. and Wood, F. (eds) *Teaching Emotionally Disturbed Children*, Boston: Little, Brown and Co.

REFERENCES

Sweiso, J. (1992) 'Discipline in schools: a concluding review', in Wheldall, K. (ed.) *Discipline in Schools: Psychological Perspectives on the Elton Report*, London: Routledge.

Szasz, T.S. (1960) 'The myth of mental illness', *American Psychologist*, 15, 113–18.

Szasz, T.S. (1972) *The Myth of Mental Illness*, St Albans: Paladin.

Tattum, D.P. (1982) *Disruptive Pupils in Schools and Units*, Chichester: Wiley.

Tattum, D.P. (1986) 'Consistency management – school and classroom concerns and issues', in Tattum, D.P. (ed.) *Management of Disruptive Pupil Behaviour in Schools*, Chichester: Wiley.

Taylor, D. and Dowling, E. (1986) 'The clinic goes to school: setting up an outreach service', *Maladjustment and Therapeutic Education*, 4, 2, 90–8.

Tomlinson, S. (1982) *A Sociology of Special Education*, London: Routledge and Kegan Paul.

Topping, K. (1992) 'Cooperative learning and peer tutoring, an overview', *The Psychologist*, 5, 151–61.

Tyler, K. (1992) 'The development of the ecosystemic approach as a humanistic educational psychology', *Educational Psychology*, 12, 1, 15–24.

Upton, G. (1981) 'The early years controversy and its implications for working with maladjusted children', *New Growth*, 1, 2, 11–20.

Upton, G. and Cooper, P. (1990) 'A new perspective on behaviour problems in schools: the ecosystemic approach', *Maladjustment and Therapeutic Education*, 8, 1, 3–18.

Varma, V.P. (ed.) (1990) *The Management of Children with Emotional and Behaviour Difficulties*, London: Routledge.

von Bertalanffy, L. (1950) 'The theory of open systems in physics and biology', *Science*, 3, 25–9.

von Bertalanffy, L. (1968) *General System Theory*, New York: Brazillier.

Walker, S. (1984) *Learning Theory and Behaviour Modification*, London: Methuen.

Watzlawick, P. (1984) *The Invented Reality*, New York: W.W. Norton.

Watzlawick, P., Weakland, J. and Fisch, R. (1974) *Change: Principles of Problem Formation and Resolution*, New York: Norton.

West, D. and Farrington, D. (1973) *Who Becomes Delinquent?* London: Heinemann.

Wheldall, K. (1987) *The Behaviourist in the Classroom*, London: Allen and Unwin.

Wheldall, K. and Entwistle, J. (1988) 'Back in the USSR: the effect of teacher modelling of silent reading on pupils' reading behaviour in the primary school classroom', *Educational Psychology*, 8, 51–66.

Wheldall, K. and Glynn, T. (1988) 'Contingencies in contexts: a behavioural interactionist perspective in education', *Educational Psychology*, 8, 5–19.

Wheldall, K. and Glynn, T. (1989) *Effective Classroom Learning: A Behavioural Interactionist Approach to Teaching*, London: Basil Blackwell.

Wheldall, K. and Merrett, F. (1984) *Positive Teaching: The Behavioural Approach*, London: Allen and Unwin.

Wheldall, K. and Merrett, F. (1992) 'Effective classroom behaviour management: positive teaching', in Wheldall, K. (ed.) *Discipline in Schools: Psychological Perspectives on the Elton Report*, London: Routledge.

Wheldall, K. and Olds, D. (1987) 'Of sex and seating: the effects of mixed and same sex seating arrangements in junior classroom', *New Zealand Journal of Educational Studies*, 22, 71-85.

Wheldall, K., Bevan, K. and Shortall, K. (1986) 'A touch of reinforcement: the effects of contingent teacher touch on the classroom behaviour of young children', *Educational Review*, 38, 207–16.

Wheldall, K., Morris, M., Vaughan, P. and Ng, Y.Y. (1981) 'Rows versus tables: an example of the use of behaviour ecology in two classes of eleven-year-old children', *Educational Psychology*, 1, 171–84.

Wheldall, K., Wheldall, D. and Winter, S. (1983) *Seven Supertactics for Superparents*, Windsor: NFER/Nelson.

Whyte, L.L. (1962) *The Unconscious before Freud*, London: Tavistock Publications.

Widlake, P. (1983) *How to Reach the Hard to Teach*, Milton Keynes: Open University Press.

Williams, J. and Weeks, G. (1984) 'The use of paradoxical techniques in a school setting', *The American Journal of Family Therapy*, 12, 3, 47–57.

Wills, D. (1960) *Throw Away Thy Rod*, London: Victor Gollancz.

Wilson, M. and Evans, M. (1980) *Education of Disturbed Pupils*, London: Methuen.

Winnicott, D.W. (1965) *The Maturational Process and the Facilitating Environment*, London: Hogarth Press.

Winnicott, D.W. (1977) *The Piggle*, Harmondsworth: Penguin.

Wolfgang, C.H. and Glickman, C.D. (1986) *Solving Discipline Problems: Strategies for Classroom Teachers*, Boston: Allyn and Bacon.

Woods, P. (1976) 'Having a laugh: an antidote to schooling', in Hammersley, M. and Woods, P. (eds) *The Process of Schooling*, London, Routledge and Kegan Paul.

Woods, P. (1979) *The Divided School*, Milton Keynes: Open University Press.

Woods, P. (1990a) *Teacher Skills and Strategies*, Lewes: Falmer Press.

Woods, P. (1990b) *The Happiest Days, How Pupils Cope with Schools*, Lewes: Falmer Press.

Worden, M. (1981) 'Classroom behavior as a function of the family system', *The School Counsellor*, 8, 3, 178–88.

Wragg, E.C. (1984) 'Teaching skills', in Wragg, E.C. (ed.) *Classroom Teaching Skills*, Beckenham: Croom Helm.

Wragg, E.C. and Wood, E.K. (1984) 'Pupil appraisal of teaching', in Wragg, E.C. (ed.) *Classroom Teaching Skills*, Beckenham: Croom Helm.

AUTHOR INDEX

203

SUBJECT INDEX